Angel Power

Angel Power

Janice T. Connell

With a Foreword by Father Robert Faricy

Ballantine Books

New York

Grateful acknowledgment is made to the following for permission to reprint previously published material:

Christian Classics: Excerpts from the *Summa Theologiae* by Thomas Aquinas (Concise Edition, ed. by Timothy McDermott, 1989) and *The Angels and Their Mission* by Jean Danielou, S.J. (1957) are reprinted with permission from the publisher, Christian Classics, a division of Thomas More, 200 East Bethany Drive, Allen, Texas 75002.

Tan Books & Publishers, Inc.: Excerpts from *A Tour of the Summa* by Msgr. Paul J. Glenn.

United States Catholic Conference: Scripture selections are taken from the *New American Bible*. Copyright © 1991, 1986, 1970 by the Confraternity of Christian Doctrine, Washington, DC, and are used with permission. All rights reserved.

Newsweek: Excerpt from *Newsweek*, March 3, 1989, Newsweek, Inc. All rights reserved. Reprinted by permission.

DECLARATION

The decree of the Congregation for the Propagation of the Faith, A.A.S. 58, 1186 (approved by Pope Paul VI on 14 October 1966) states that the *Nihil Obstat* and *Imprimatur* are no longer required on publications that deal with private revelations, provided that they contain nothing contrary to faith and morals. The author wishes to manifest her unconditional submission to the final and official judgment of the Magisterium of the Church in matters of faith and morals.

Library of Congress Catalog Card Number: 94-94563
ISBN:0-345-39123-3

Text design by Holly Johnson
Cover design by Judy Herbstman
Cover painting: *Angels Dancing Before the Sun*, courtesy of Giraudon/Art Resource. Background photo © Telegraph Colour Library/FPG Int'l.
Photo research by Omni Photo Communications.

Manufactured in the United States of America

First Edition: March 1995

10 9 8 7 6 5 4 3 2 1

This book is consecrated to God in thanksgiving for the angels.
It is dedicated to the Eternal Father.

Contents

❦

Acknowledgments

The Nine Choirs of Angels.

All who treasure the mystery of inexhaustible Truth.

People throughout the world who toil tirelessly to live and spread the work of the angels.

My family, who provided the inspiration that gave life to this joyous book.

Joëlle Delbourgo, whose wisdom guided its pages.

Leigh Ann Sackrider, for her graciousness and expertise.

Marcy Posner and Matthew Bialer.

Countless friends of the angels from around the world, who have personally helped on this project but in their humility have chosen to remain anonymous.

Author's Note

Spiritual experiences are very private, personal events that happen in the lives of all people. The stories in this book are compilations of true stories of individuals, some of whom are public figures and other notable persons, who have shared with me their extraordinary encounters with the angels. Their names and some of the circumstances have been changed to protect their privacy.

Foreword

Do you believe in angels? Do you believe that angels exist? Perhaps you do. Perhaps you do not. Perhaps you do not know whether they exist or not, or what they might be.

Have you experienced the presence or the help of angels? Maybe you have. Or maybe you have had some experience of evil spirits, of demons, perhaps of a bad spirit masquerading as an angel of light, as they can do. Many people have had such experiences, encounters of one kind or another with angels, the good spirits, or with bad spirits, or with both.

This book is about angels.

Angels are real, part of reality. Angels are not mythical beings, nor are they personifications of psychological or social forces or drives. Angels are not projections of the human unconscious mind. They are not abstractions. And they do not belong to primitive or outmoded ways of thinking.

Angels are persons; they have their own personalities and characteristics. There are many, many angels, more than there are human beings. They stand before the throne of God and praise Him. At the same time, they are among us, with us.

Angels are real. And they are here.

Since the beginning of human history most religions have recognized the existence and the importance of spiritual creatures. In some religions the distinction between good spirits or angels on the one hand, and bad spirits or demons on the other hand, has remained unclear. Other religions have taken account of evil spirits, but for the most part ignored angels.

But the religions of western civilization, especially Islam, Christianity, Zoroastrianism, and Judaism, bring out the important differences between good and evil spirits, between angels and demons. They understand that angels are with God, from God, work for God, that they are good, that they are powerful—much more powerful than bad spirits—and that they are with us and for us.

Jan Connell knows about angels. In this book she tells us about them, and she shows us why they are important to the world, to every group of people, and to each one of us individually. We can learn from her the meaning of angels for our lives.

Robert Faricy
Rome, Italy
January 8th, 1995

Preface

Humanity stands at the brink of the Era of Angels. A spiritual awakening unlike anything known in the history of the world begins now. This book is for all those who desire to know angels well and to communicate with them. Angel Power is a source of empowerment by which even the smallest and weakest human being can ascend to the heights of peace, joy, and love. Angel Power is the energy to ascend to God's Kingdom. Those who ride on the wings of the angels ride in the arms of God. Now is a glorious time for those who know the angels well.

The wisdom of the ages teaches that each individual, whether believer or not, good or bad, old or young, sick or well, rich or poor, has a personal Guardian Angel with him or her at every moment of life's journey. Our personal Guardian Angel stands by, day and night, waiting to serve us, bless us, and help us for the glory of God and to bring peace to His People on earth. There are also other kinds of angels, in addition to Guardian Angels, each of whom is well equipped to provide power, courage, strength, wisdom, consolation, understanding, and knowledge. Holy angels bring the very strength and power of God to all those who sincerely invite them into their lives.

We access Angel Power by being consciously aware of the presence of the

angels and by communicating with them. All people are meant to enjoy and share the unconditional love of the Nine Choirs of Angels. Angel Power is a source of joy, peace, abundance, and great love for all who receive it.

Those who know how to access the power of angels experience great blessings and immense happiness. Angel Power is accessible to everyone of goodwill. However, Angel Power will not help us to get our own way unless our cause is just. Angel Power is not a means to further mere human capriciousness. Rather, Angel Power achieves the fulfillment of our choices that bring glory to God and blessings upon ourselves and one another.

Most people, in the deepest part of their memory, hold the angels in great esteem. The angels are quite powerful and do make themselves known. For thousands of years people all over the world have believed in angels. Some found them inexplicable; others have been quite conscious of the angels and have lived in close harmony with them.

My own quest for the angels began when I was visited by a tragedy as a small child. In the midst of that terror something very beautiful happened: I was rescued by the angels. That encounter when I was two years old has led me along the paths of life with an absolute certitude about the presence and reality of Angel Power. The purpose of this book is to share some of the insights and stories I have learned that are interwoven in the tapestry of humanity's journey with the angels.

Everyone needs angels. Angels are intertwined in the events and circumstances of ordinary people caught up in the business of daily obligations. The angels constantly do extraordinary things for ordinary people. The angels love each of us individually and unconditionally under all circumstances. The angels, who are always with us, are channels of Divine Love. Pure spirits, they are neither male nor female. Angels are as numerous as the stars in the sky. Though they are everywhere, they are usually invisible. Angels carry God's Unconditional Love to all people.

Angels are God's Ambassadors to the planet Earth. People who are consciously aware of the presence of the angels realize they are surrounded by an invisible armada of pure spirits of unconditional love. These blessed spirits are armed with the authority and might of Paradise. Angels bring human beings the power to transcend the limitations of space and time. Angels also bring healing, perseverance, creativity, fortitude, joy, and solutions to the problems and circumstances of our human conditions.

Angels surround all people and events. They ennoble and enrich all people. Angels experience immense joy in serving God's children. They long for us to assign them tasks and projects. Sweetness of life surrounds those who access Angel Power. Those who do not yet live in harmony with the angels in seeking solutions to the miseries of the earth suffer needlessly.

More and more people all over the world are awakening to the presence of angels. As such awareness is heightened and refined, the hope is that people will permit angels to bring Divine Remedies to the mistakes and problems of our times. It gives angels great joy to be included in human pursuits that hasten the coming of the Kingdom of God on earth. People who learn to access angels and to rely upon their power find one of the greatest treasures of creation.

Angels, always present and aware of our needs, are most humble. They do not interfere in our lives unless we invite them to do so. They usually communicate with us in the silence of our interior understanding: we "hear" angels with our hearts. They communicate their messages directly to our intelligence so that we understand them clearly.

During a particularly difficult and trying time in my personal life, certain members of my family and a few close friends began to notice some of the graciousness that I attributed to the angels who guided me in the dark night of faith. Gradually people of all walks of life, levels of education, and differing beliefs, and some with no professed faith at all, were asking me for information about Angel Power. Subsequently I was invited to lecture at national and international congresses, conferences, conventions, clubs, seminars, churches, synagogues, radio shows, and even on television documentaries about contemporary issues and the power of the angels to help all of us in our daily lives.

Angels bring solutions, strength, and power to those who sincerely invite them into their lives. All people on earth have been created to enjoy and share the unconditional love of the Nine Choirs of Angels. Angel Power is a source of lasting joy and enlightenment for all who receive it.

Wherever you are on your own journey with angels, I trust that some of the facts, stories, and secrets you will find in these pages will add great happiness to your life, especially since we stand on the threshold of the Era of Holy Angels that has been prophesied since the beginning and is contained in the sacred texts. The curtain begins even now to rise as the mystery of angels unfolds before our eyes.

In researching Angel Power I have relied on the teachings of Saint Gregory the Great, who saw spiritual belief not merely as a quest for the mysterious but as a personal encounter with the Divine. The *Summa Theologica* of the great Angelic Doctor, Saint Thomas Aquinas, provides the fabric for *Angel Power.*

The Meditations and Prayers I have written for this book are presented as a suggested guide for our odyssey with angels, though I suspect the angels themselves will teach you how to speak to them as you become proficient in accessing Angel Power. The Meditations and Prayers are simply intended as possibilities for experiences along the path of enlightenment, consolation, endurance, petition, gratitude, and Divine Adoration. A few of the more famous Prayers that have been used throughout the ages in addressing angels are also included.

This book is offered in the hope that the experiences it describes will be a source of inspiration and a tool for everyone to access Angel Power. It is given with much gratitude and love.

Wonderful stories about the marvelous things angels have done for our grandparents, great-grandparents, and ancestors are a special legacy of many families. Angels manifest themselves to each of us, often in mysterious ways. The behavior of the angels presented in these pages is rooted in true stories. In certain personal stories names, places, or some of the circumstances have been changed to protect the privacy of those who have so graciously shared their encounters. Of great significance is the fact that many of the stories, though they span nations and generations, are similar.

Often, painful situations that people find particularly onerous provide challenging opportunities to reach a higher level of consciousness and a deeper awareness of the reality of the spiritual world. Bad times create good spiritual growth if awareness is coupled with faith in a higher power and humility to use the tools of the higher power. Angels are inseparable friends, who bring strength and consolation to those who include them in their lives. In truth, angels are our best friends.

The invisible world of holy angels belongs to us. Most of the time we do not enter into the world of angels. They are brilliantly humble. Angels in general do not directly interfere in our lives unless we invite them. But there are exceptions to that rule! Though it is usually not their way, if you should suddenly discover an angel meddling in your life, be prepared. When an angel arrives on the scene, amazing things happen.

Angel Insurance Policy

Many people purchase property insurance, health insurance, and car insurance. They do not want to be stranded in times of unforeseen misfortune. Why not an Angel Insurance Policy rooted in Angel Power? Angel Power is a free gift of God available to everyone. An Angel Insurance Policy will give you a blessed hedge against the unforeseen.

Angels are real. They help all people on earth in millions of unrecognized ways every day. You have a personal Guardian Angel assigned to you by God. Do you know your Guardian Angel? You can be quite certain that your Guardian Angel knows you better than you know yourself. Your Guardian Angel, who is of superior capacity and vision, knows the consequences that attach to many of your life decisions even though you do not. Your Guardian Angel has the power to help you make the best choice possible in any given situation so that the outcome of your life decisions will bear great blessings for yourself and others if you access Angel Power.

Take a risk. Give yourself an Angel Insurance Policy.

Speak to your Guardian Angel in the privacy of your heart. Ask, right now, that your invisible Guardian Angel become known to you in whatever way you most need. If you are sincere, be assured that you shall come to know your Guardian Angel and many of the countless angels of the Celestial Court as you read *Angel Power*.

You and your Guardian Angel are a powerful team. As you learn to depend more and more on Angel Power, the vicissitudes of life on earth become a glorious journey into the land of the living, where you recognize what a masterpiece of God's love you really are.

Angel Power

Prologue

I Am the Great God of Abraham.
I Am the Faithful One.
I have assigned My Angels to guard each of you.
To access the power of My Angels, you must hear My Voice.
To hear My Voice, you must pray.
To Pray, you must trust.
To trust My Power, you must love Me.
To love Me, you must know Me.
To know Me, you must seek Me.
To seek Me is to find Me.
All else passes away but My Will.
I live in the heart of all creation.
I am Life.

Part I

The Power of the Angels

＊＊＊

See, I am sending an angel before you, to guard you on the way
 and bring you to the place I have prepared.
Be attentive to him and heed his voice.

Do not rebel against him, for he will not forgive your sin.

My authority resides in him.
If you heed his voice and carry out all I tell you, I will be an enemy
 to your enemies and a foe to your foes.

—EXODUS 23:20

Chapter One

The Truth About Angels

At present we see indistinctly, as in a mirror . . .
—1 CORINTHIANS 13:12

Angels are usually invisible to the human eye, but not to the human heart. They fill the heavens, the cosmos, and the earth. Scholars throughout the ages have taught that all angels are grouped into nine different Choirs in ascending levels of power and authority. Each Choir is a group of angels with the same mission. These Nine Choirs are grouped into three classes, each containing three groups.[1]

The highest class of angels is known as the Angels of Pure Contemplation. These are the Seraphim, Cherubim, and Thrones. They possess, in descending order, the highest degrees of knowledge and awareness of God. The Seraphim

Divinity: Uncreated Energy

CREATION: CREATED ENERGY

The Nine Choirs of Angels

ANGELS OF PURE CONTEMPLATION
Govern All Creation

    1. Seraphim

    2. Cherubim

    3. Thrones

ANGELS OF THE COSMOS
Govern All the Cosmos

    4. Dominions

    5. Powers

    6. Virtues

ANGELS OF THE WORLD
Govern All the World

    7. Principalities

    8. Archangels

    9. Angels

are the most gifted of all angels, followed by the Cherubim, and then the Thrones.[2]

The middle class of angels, the Angels of the Cosmos, contains the Dominions, Powers, and Virtues. Their power is received from the Angels of Pure Contemplation, especially the Thrones. (The Seraphim and the Cherubim, so exquisitely close to the Divine Presence of God, personally draw near few creatures.) The Angels of the Cosmos distribute, in descending order of intensity, the power and instructions they receive from the Angels of Pure Contemplation.[3]

The lowest class of angels, the Angels of the World, is composed of the Principalities, the Archangels, and the Angels. They contain power transmitted to them from the Angels of the Cosmos, and in turn they disburse the power they receive, in a descending order of intensity, to the earth. They receive their instructions from the Angels of the Cosmos.[4]

All the angels of the entire Nine Choirs are actively engaged in the mission of helping humans gain entrance to the Kingdom of Heaven. When the world ends, that particular mission of the Nine Choirs of Angels will be complete.[5]

Each angel in the Nine Choirs is unique, perfectly glorious, exquisitely humble, and astonishingly beautiful. The angels always come where they are properly invited. They bring great blessings into our lives. We drive their protection away by unloving thoughts and deeds. We draw the angels back into our lives by being truly sorry for our poor choices. Holy angels have the strength and the wisdom and the power and the means to help us live happy, productive, contented, love-filled lives of peace and joy and abundance.

Angels are living replicas of God's Divine Love, Power, and Beauty. They are pure spirits of harmony and peace created by God before the world began. God is uncreated energy, since all flows from God as the Source. The angels, spirits who flow from God's Love, are bits of created energy.

Love is energy. Power is energy. Beauty is energy. Angels bear within their essence the energy of love, power, and beauty. They are the agents of God assigned to each one of us as His Consolers, His Messengers, even His Chastisers (Isaiah 37:36).

People of goodwill long to know angels, to enjoy their presence, power, and protection. The experience is quite personal and different for each person. Some individuals throughout history have possessed a deep knowledge of angels. What is their secret? Such knowledge is a Divine Gift of God's Love. It is offered to everyone.

Angels see everything on earth, under the earth, in the depths of the seas, in the skies, and in the entire universe. They watch every event and listen to every word that is spoken, too. They are not, however, permitted to access our private thoughts. It is God who reads the hearts of His children of the earth. (We have the freedom to ask God to allow our Guardian Angel and all the other angels to know our thoughts.)

The cosmic laws are managed by angels. Angels are quite capable of changing any of the cosmic laws in a split second. The power of angels is so great that any angel is capable of stopping a comet in an instant. The angels derive their power from God, so nothing is beyond their strength. The earth, too, is managed by angels. Their job is to bring order out of chaos.[6] (Chaos is the trademark of the powers of darkness.)

Angels are quite aware that our time on earth is short. Eternity is forever. Angels constantly seek to prepare us for our journey into eternity. They inspire us to pray in whatever way we can. They encourage us to abandon ourselves to God's Providence in their care. They want us to allow ourselves to belong totally to God. His Love for us is unconditional and unchanging. The angels know that it is we who run from God. God never abandons us: we abandon God—His Angels, His Ways, His Will.

Angels constantly warn us not to worry about anything but God's Will, for they know that God's Will is a personal path of peace, joy, and love that He has uniquely designed for each of us. They always inspire us to pray more, to sacrifice the fleeting things. They want us to simplify our lives and eliminate needless things, especially worry. Worry is lack of trust in Angel Power and in God's Ability to make all things well. (God comes to us when we least expect it.) His Will for us is perfect happiness. The angels want us to hear God and see God.

God is always present in the heavens and throughout the cosmos and the earth. He surrounds us with His Love. God fills our world with joyous angels. We are never alone. God wants us to know His Angels as our playmates and confidantes. He has assigned them the task of guarding us from the malevolence that swirls about the cosmos and the earth.

Angel Power communicates Truth, which brings the blessings and bounty of God. To access the power of the holy angels requires prayer, fasting, meditation, silence, and selflessness. Those who access the angels travel with Angel Power. They become filled with heroism and self-sacrifice (Luke

22:43–46). When Angel Power rules, the Earth is a holy and very happy place in which to live.

Angels are most helpful companions when we choose to pray and fast for a higher purpose than our own physical appetites and cravings. The angels strengthen and enlighten us to comprehend that those who do not fast cannot know God. Voluntary fasting is a sign of kinship with God. Fasting means abstinence from various pleasures and activities, not for the purpose of suffering but to strengthen ourselves or to help others. Ultimately fasting is a way of showing God that we love Him more than the person, place, or thing from which we abstain. It is pleasing to God to see His children fast from sinful places, sinful situations, sinful sensual experiences. The angels help us to recognize that freedom from illusion requires us to fast with our eyes, our tongue, our hands, our feet, our ears. Through fasting, our will bends to the breath of God.

All angels receive their being and knowledge and power from God. It is the knowledge and power of God that they bring to us. Angelic knowledge is steeped in wisdom and grace. Angels do not have sense knowledge as we do. They have intellectual knowledge, which is more effective than our knowledge because it is not dependent upon mere sensual communication. Angels do not know that something is hot by feeling it, for they have no bodies that would feel the heat. Rather they know intellectually that something is hot or cold. They instantly comprehend the most complex constituency of all matter.[7]

Our private thoughts are known only to God. The secret thoughts of all of us are not known by angels or demons or one another. Every prayer, however, is heard instantly by our Guardian Angel. A prayer operates like a powerful beam of light that shines on our Guardian Angel's intellect as it ascends to the Throne of God. Our behavior and our spoken words are always observed and heard by angels.

Evil spirits, too, are prowling about at all times. They do not have access to Divine Wisdom or Grace. Demonic knowledge is steeped in error and falsehood.[8] Demons can make their thoughts and wishes known to one another and to humans.

The absolute truth is that the nearer to Almighty God an angelic or human being draws, the greater that being's power over other creatures. Therefore, the good angels rule and control the demons.[9] The more we consciously seek God and toil to comply with His Loving Will for us, the easier it is to hear good angels. The more we bend our wills to the inspirations of good angels, the happier and more peace-filled we become, for we ascend on the wings of God's Love out of the brokenness of the human condition.

God has empowered angels to lead us away from deceptions that would ensnare us, that would steal our peace, joy, love, and tranquility. Angels are a gift to us from God. No one has to accept a gift. We have the choice to allow holy angels to lead us or not. We give the angels great pleasure when we recognize them and follow their gentle inspirations. Angels desire to draw us into the very Heart of God.

God wishes to dwell in each person on the earth (John 15:23). Though we are made of the dust of the earth, having a clay vessel for a body, the raging fires of Divinity desire to burn in each human. The essential nature of angels and humans allows us to know God.[10] Our journey on the earth is surrounded with enlightened angels of the Nine Choirs, who have the Divine Assignment to guard us and guide us to our Heavenly Home. Those who come to know the angels access the very power and love of God.

The Bible identifies the Nine Choirs of Angels and is filled with the works of holy angels in the lives of humans. The Prophets identify the Seraphim and Cherubim (2 Kings 19:15; Ezekiel 9:3; Psalms 18:11, 24:7–8). Saint Paul speaks of Principalities, Powers, Virtues, Dominions, and Thrones (Ephesians 1:21; Colossians 1:16). The Angels and Archangels complete the glories of the Nine Choirs.

From the beginning of recorded history there are indications that the various peoples of the earth have believed in angels and other invisible beings, or in a Being who holds some authority and control over the visible world: the Babylonians, the Chaldeans, the Egyptians, the ancient Jews, the Persians, the Africans and Middle Eastern peoples, the Indians, the ancient Chinese and other Asian peoples, the Native Americans, the Europeans.[11] From one end of the earth to the other, rituals and rules have sprung up among the different peoples in response to beliefs that motivate their behavior in relationship to the invisible world.

According to a *Newsweek* poll conducted in March of 1989, 94 percent of all Americans believe that God exists; 77 percent believe in Heaven. Moreover,

76 percent believe they have a good or excellent chance of going to Heaven after death; 91 percent believe Heaven is a place of great peace; 83 percent believe they will be with God in Heaven.

Those who believe in God believe in angels. Modern telecommunications now transmit these beliefs to the global community. International, intercultural spiritual beliefs permeate the winds of the earth.

Angel Power Brings Heaven on Earth

Bless the Lord, all you angels, mighty in strength and attentive, obedient to every command . . .

—PSALMS 103:20

Those who are enlightened bless all that comes upon the path that must be traveled in the course of a lifetime. They bless and love so that the sweetness of God's Ways may be tasted. God's Ways are Heaven on earth. Soon His Earth will be pure again. His children will experience Heaven on earth as they love and bless one another.

Burning gas lines and eerie fires sent shivers throughout the entire television world as the city of angels, Los Angeles, awakened on the morning of January 17, 1994. A mere eighteen-second earthquake had crumbled buildings and homes like papier-mâché; destroyed vital parts of the freeway system, creating a snarled wasteland of vehicles with no place to go; knocked out phone and electric lines; ruptured water pipes and devastated the livelihood of many inhabitants of the second largest city in America. Preliminary estimates of the financial damage alone were projected to reach as high as seventy billion dollars. The extent of the emotional, psychological, and physical hardships for Los Angeles residents who withstood the earthquake may not be known this side of Paradise. The suddenness of the catastrophe affected the world. Earthquakes spare nothing.

Earthquakes are great teachers. They communicate powerfully that the purpose of human life is to love. Catastrophe allows us to see one another in a new light. God's Light. Earthquakes remind humankind not to build castles in the "sands of illusion." As we have learned from the ancient Pharaohs of Egypt, who stored up their earthly treasures in their Pyramid tombs, nothing of the earth that we build, acquire, or use belongs to us or will go with us when our time to leave the earth arrives. No person escapes the process of life that forces us ever onward toward our eternal destiny. We all truly live and die as pilgrims on the earth, journeying home beyond the five senses, where we no longer need our bodies or things of the earth. In the meantime all the beautiful things of the earth are God's Gifts to us, but only for a while. We can possess or keep nothing. Earthquakes allow us to see our lives against the wider horizon of the mystery of God's Providence and His Divine Plan for each of us.

People wince when their life choices and human accomplishments are crushed in the winepress of God's Will. However, nothing happens that He does not allow. Those who hear His Voice live in peace because they trust His

Love and His Providential Care for each of His children.

God is Graciousness. He requires that His children become gracious too. God's Graciousness accommodates the weakness of all His children. His Graciousness is silence when He is not asked. God's Graciousness is absence when He is not invited. His Graciousness forbears when His children seek to exploit His Graciousness. God withholds rewards from those who abuse His Graciousness.

All the lovely things of the earth are a gift from God to His children. The difficult, painful things are permitted by Him and are used to allow us the dignity of growth in love and faithfulness.

Love is eternal. The mystery of love is perfected by personal faithfulness to God's Will. Those who love find eternal life.

LOVE IS ETERNAL

Love without faith and hope is weak. It is feeble.
Love without faith and hope is a victim of fear.
Love grounded in faith in God's Word,
Hope in His Promises,
Casts out all fear.

Love grounded in man's faith, and man's hope is self-love.

Self-love is transitory, like all things of the earth.
It is fragile and easily collapses.
Pride is the father of self-love.
Ego is the mother of self-love.
When pride and ego combine, self-love builds artificial villages on the
sands of deception.

The Pacific Rim is called the Rim of Fire, for it is constantly subject to earthquakes. Earthquakes awaken humans from illusion. Illusion is the snare that leads humans into deception. Illusion mocks Truth. Illusion is counterfeit.

There was a merciful component to the Los Angeles earthquake of 1994. The quake hit the city of angels at 4:31 A.M., when few people were out and about. If the freeways had been packed with rush-hour commuters, the death toll could have been macabre. Holy angels were watching over the inhabitants of the city named for the angels.

Thinking people are rightfully reticent about ascribing supernatural causes to natural disasters. Few have problems recognizing that God, however one defines that indefinable word, speaks through the ordinary circumstances of day-to-day life. Was the earthquake a warning to mankind that mere human power is basically nothing?

Angels bring the blessings and rewards of God to His Faithful People. They also mete out the fiery judgment of God upon people, places, and things as a means of awakening God's children.

Scripture informs us that angels do inflict God's Chastisements. Zacharias became mute because he doubted the authenticity of the angel's announcement concerning his elderly wife Elizabeth's pregnancy with John the Baptist (Luke 1:20). Angels are recorded in the sacred texts as God's executioners. One hundred eighty-five thousand men were slain by an angel of the Lord in the Assyrian camp (2 Kings 19:35; Isaiah 37:36).

Not all spiritual forces are good. There are evil forces in the cosmos and on earth whose presence and power can lead the unwary to tragedy. The agenda of that evil force is to seduce human beings into depravity, destruction, despair, and finally death. A fierce battle rages between the often invisible forces of good and evil. The booty is human souls.

No event occurs in the heavens, throughout the cosmos, or on earth except by the permission of God.[12] The Psalms tell us that *"Whatever the Lord wishes he does in heaven and on earth, in the seas and in all the deeps,"* (Psalm 135:6). The Patriarchs, Prophets, and Doctors of the church have consistently taught that nothing happens without God willing and allowing it. Evil is the only exception. Though never willed by God, evil is permitted. Evil is action devoid of God. For reasons that at present are obscure, evil is the quintessential mystery, out of which God promises to bring good.

Saint Augustine grappled with a life of good and evil, poverty and riches, sickness and health, natural disaster and tranquility. He pondered deeply the punishment meted out by God to King David for the murder and adultery he committed (2 Samuel 12:7–12). Augustine concluded,

All that happens to us in this world against our will (whether
due to men or to other causes) happens to us only by the will
of God, by the disposal of Providence, by His orders and under His guidance: and if by the frailty of our understanding
we cannot grasp the reason for some event, let us attribute it
to Divine Providence, show Him respect by accepting it from
His hand, believe firmly that He does not send it to us without cause.[13]

Nothing happens by coincidence. Angel Power serves as a trumpet blast
to the forces of nature. Angel Power summons the cosmic laws to rise up in
majesty and assert divinely ordained order. Natural disaster can therefore be
viewed perhaps as a message and an invitation.

Evil forces contrive incessantly to deprive humans of the experience of
love, peace, and joy. Illicit drugs, weapons, political oppressions, and even the
raging sounds of some man-made music often send human awareness and sensitivity into the realms of unconsciousness. Whenever and wherever humans
are unconscious, the forces of evil are capable of usurping human freedom.

Shocking headlines in 1991 and 1992 announced the existence of concentration camps in the region where World War I began. The memory of the
Sarajevo Winter Olympics had hardly faded when starving people were pho-
tographed and televised as they froze to death during the winters of 1993 and
1994. Telecommunications carried the holocaust of civil war in Bosnia to the

eyes of the world. The atrocities were mocking voices defying the good intentions of the rest of the world.

In less than a week more than one hundred thousand people were slaughtered in Rwanda as violent civil war exploded out of the hearts of some of the people in the spring of 1994. Headlines announced HELL ON EARTH, and millions died in Rwanda during the summer of 1994.[14] Telecommunications brought the brutality to the viewing audience of the world. Why does such inhuman behavior occur? Why is it tolerated? How can such brutality be stopped? Those who are unconscious feel nothing. They do nothing.

The HIV virus, which causes AIDS, was identified in 1981. Since then it has sent its icy fingers of death down the spines of men, women, and children all over the world. No one has yet been able to develop a cure for AIDS. It holds its victims captive. Other illnesses do so as well. Scientists have learned that many antibiotics are no longer capable of eliminating the dreaded bacterial infections that at one time wiped out populations of entire cities.[15] Medical methods are unequal to the virulence of mutant bacteria and enigmatic viruses that threaten everyone.

The entire world watches suffering. Every city has the disease of violent crime. Hospitals are filled with pain and despair. Some people see the suffering that is all around us; others are oblivious to its presence.

Evil forces have sown the seeds of suffering from generation to generation. Suffering is clothed as a beggar. Few welcome it. Few respect it. Few understand it. Suffering is a patient and relentless teacher. It has lived in every generation. Suffering knows no geographic, racial, or economic bounds. Often it shows up when it is least expected. God permits suffering. Why?

Nothing is hidden from the face of God. No act of an angel or human, good or bad, is hidden from Him. The angels know that God is always present in the heavens, the cosmos, and on earth. Nothing escapes His Gaze. Suffering and bliss, war and peace, riches and poverty, sickness and health are permitted by God to exist side by side. When we are able to bless every act and circumstance of our lives, as God has asked us all to do, we acknowledge His Presence and His Lordship. When we curse any person, place, or thing, we ourselves become profane. We are not living in truth.

God alone is Truth. The angels, tested spirits of pure Truth, long to draw near to us so that, through them, we may draw nearer to the Living God. Those who draw nearer to the Living God begin to comprehend Truth. Truth alone frees humans from bondage.

God sees everything in an eternal present. He sees us as we were, as we are, and as we will be. It is we who do not yet have eyes to behold the wonders of God. There is no past or future. All is always before the face of God. Angels are aware that all will be well. They desire to help us see the same. Angels carry the light of Truth to us.

Those who awaken to the conscious presence of God in, around, and about all that exists gradually become aware of Truth. To surrender into the conscious awareness of the presence of God is to acknowledge Him. Those who give every thought, word, and deed to God learn to live in humble acceptance of His Presence in the world. They begin to hear Truth sing of the reality that all belongs to God. Spiritual awakening cures human blindness to God's Presence in the world.

The great mystery and challenge is that evil and sin are always present too. They are part of the world in which we now live. Since God is pure love, power, and beauty, the existence of evil and its ugliness is a great sign of God's unconditional love for us and His Trust in us that we will overcome all the wretchedness of evil. By allowing us free will to grapple with evil, God gives each of us the possibility of entering heroic depths of love and faithfulness. Those who confront the ugliness of evil surrounded with conscious awareness of Angel Power are clothed in God's Word, God's Strength, God's Promises.

Those who sincerely access the power of God through the holy angels reach into the Empyrean Valleys of Paradise and draw the Kingdom of Heaven upon the earth. God wills for all His People to dwell with Him forever in His Kingdom of peace, joy, and love. No one is excluded.

Expect great things of the angels, for they draw near those who love. They are quite busy in the world bringing the kiss of God's Grace and Illumination to all those who welcome them. Angels carry the solutions to the great, impenetrable quandaries of our times. They are modest, hidden, and eternally gracious. Angels are spirits of tested virtue. They usually do not interfere in our lives unless they are personally invited. Those people who are kissed by the angels develop eyes to see God in the world, ears to hear Him in the world, and gradually they receive new hearts filled with peace, joy, and eternal love.

A human being who is aware that he or she lives in the presence of God, that every thought, word, and deed occurs before His Face, becomes a channel of God's Love. Such a person becomes one with the angels as God's agent and plenipotentiary to others.

Meditation

I ALONE AM.

Suffering is My Gift to My Beloved children.
Do not seek suffering. Do not refuse suffering.

Every gift from My Hand purifies.
Only purity may live in My Presence.
All else passes away.
I alone am life.

I am freeing My children from their coffins of selfishness.
I am reinfusing their hearts with a longing for Me.

Consecration

TO THE NINE CHOIRS OF ANGELS

O Holy Angels of God,
All you blessed spirits of the sacred Nine Choirs,
You are brilliant, humble, and faithful.
Before each of you I stand, clothed in
Human weakness, hope, and longing.
This day I consecrate my life to each of you.
Bless my consecration with your love, power, and might.
Protect me as a child of God and wayfarer journeying Home.
Keep me on the path of righteousness and bring me to the
Kingdom of Heaven with you now and forever.
Amen

Chapter Two

Angels on
Assignment

✠

Lie not in wait against the home of the just man,
ravage not his dwelling place;
For the just man falls seven times and rises again,
but the wicked stumble to ruin.

—PROVERBS 24:15–16

When John Milton wrote *Paradise Lost*, he turned to the Book of Revelation in the Bible, which describes the mighty episodes of Saint Michael the Archangel and his angel cohorts who rose up to fight and conquer the rebellious legions of Satan (Revelation 12:7–8). Saint Michael the Archangel and his angel cohorts remain powerful and available to defend the people of God against the wiles of evil in the modern day.

Freedom of choice is a Herculean gift of God's Mercy with which both angels and humans are endowed. Those people who access Angel Power tap into the power, superhuman vision, and knowledge of the victorious angels of all the Nine Choirs who are assigned to guard and guide the earth pilgrimage of human beings.

Ben's Story

In Washington, D.C., Ben is revered as a man with the right connections, the right attitudes, and the right answers. Known for his humility, he is tall, quiet-spoken, better-looking than the average Washington power broker, and accepted as a man with developed spiritual values. Ben has a story:

> It really started around the middle of August 1992. About a year earlier I made a business decision to merge my business corporation with a larger firm. At that time the decision seemed wise. The experts I consulted had no doubt that the merger was an excellent strategy for my quite successful operation. A little more than a year later the situation totally reversed itself. Part of the terms of the decision involved a contract that guaranteed me employment for a specified number of years and the ability to manage the affairs of my retained clients. Out of the blue the terms were changed without my consent. I was left

powerless to guarantee the integrity of my commitments to my clients. Basically, my authority was removed.

As for legal protection based on the contracts we had entered into, it became a matter of what a jury would believe the clauses meant. I had to decide whether to live with such a status quo or to move on. It was obvious to me that I needed to make a clean break. The acquiring firm and I began a series of negotiations. I chose to take with me a portion of the practice, long-standing clients who were uncomfortable dealing with anyone but me, and to leave the rest rather than compromise the integrity of my commitment. That decision seemed like the right thing to do.

What I thought were amicable discussions rapidly deteriorated into a most difficult situation. It got to the point that certain demands were made. If I didn't agree immediately, I was told to have my attorneys talk to the firm's attorneys. That of course was the "kiss of death" for me and my clients. My unfortunate position was that the firm I confronted was the single most significant one in the world in that area of business and politics. I was the classic David facing Goliath. Young David at least had a slingshot. I found myself with nothing but my moral values. I had no means of negotiating, even though in good faith, against all the resources the firm brought to bear against me. Token, sporadic negotiations proceeded throughout the summer. Issues became murkier. A massive power squeeze to destroy all my interests was in the making, and I knew it. There was nothing I could do to prevent it.

Fall came and went. We kept getting farther apart. As the end of the year arrived, we had not come to an agreement about my equity, although by contract I was obliged to leave the firm on December 31st. Without warning, all negotiations broke off completely. December 30th was the date to move the dispute to the courts. I did not have the personal financial resources to wage a courtroom battle for my rightful share, which included my lifetime's work.

The situation was dire for me, and I was brought to my knees. I prayed a great deal. There was nothing else I could do. I was financially down to nothing. Everything I ever worked for was turning to dust in my hands, and I was powerless to stop it. I prayed even more frequently, though I was not exactly sure how or for what to pray. There was tremendous pressure. One moment I was incredibly angry. The next, it was all I could do to keep from breaking down in tears. I don't recall sleeping at all in this period. I seemed to be praying day and night. Everything I had ever owned was disappearing in front of me and I did not understand why. I kept praying. They were prayers of desperation.

About a week before Christmas I suddenly sat up in my

bed. It was dark, the middle of the night. I had a strange sensation that something quite unusual was happening. I got out of my bed and looked at the clock. It was three A.M. Without realizing exactly why, I left my bedroom and walked down the hall. I experienced an incredible sensation. It was not that I was afraid. I knew that something extraordinary was going on. I walked into the guest bedroom.

The first thing I realized was that five angels were in the room. They were not little cherubs. They were huge warriors! I am six feet tall, and the angels were at least a foot taller than me. They were muscular, dressed in armor and carrying swords. Two of the angels were casually kneeling. Of these, one was kneeling on only one knee. His sword was resting on his knee and he held his helmet in his hand. He held a spear in his other hand. His head was down. Three other angels were standing in the posture of "soldiers at rest" to the left side of me as I entered the room. They, too, carried spears. They were dressed in armor and wore helmets. Their heads were down, too. The angels were olive-skinned, with medium-length straight black hair.

I gasped. The room seemed to be filled with light! I had no comprehension at first why these warrior angels were there. I stood there in awe and looked at them. They waited. I kept looking at the warrior angels, first one, then another. I waited.

Gradually I began to realize that the angels were waiting

for me to give them orders! These angel warriors were actually waiting for me to give them directions! I had been in the military; there is quite a difference between an officer and an enlisted man. These angels were of the caliber of high-ranking officers with large forces under their authority.

Slowly I was able to comprehend that these warrior angels were commanders of fathomless spiritual forces. These five armor-clad warriors were high-ranking angels of extraordinary authority and ability who led vast battalions of angels. It was quite clear to me that each warrior angel in front of me led enormous legions of other angels. Their power was obvious, but their holiness was at the edge of incomprehensibility. They had absolutely no fierceness. Rather, they were unlimited, abiding strength. At the same time they were sentinels of eternal love. I lapsed into a state of wonder: reverent awe. Many truths were illumined for me. An angel will never be a coconspirator in anything evil.

As I adjusted to the wonder of the angel-filled room, a peaceful courage began to fill me. I actually began to talk to the warrior angels. First I asked them why they were there. They told me they were sent to me by God at the request of my Guardian Angel. Like a coach with his team I explained the circumstances I faced: how distorted my business and financial circumstances had become. They understood. In fact they seemed to know everything. I told the angels I was not looking for any special treatment, but for equity and fairness. I asked them for help, to solve my financial problems in a just way. There was much personal enlightenment coming to me as I spoke to the angels. I felt incredible peace for the first time in my life. I began to comprehend the majesty of truth in a new light.

There was no actual discussion. The angels nodded their heads, confirming that they understood everything I was saying. Somehow as I spoke I began to realize that everyone on earth, even my worst enemy, has a personal Guardian Angel who always sees the face of God. Each Guardian Angel is able to communicate simultaneously with any other angel in the entire Celestial Court at any time. In that light, that new understanding, I actually instructed the angel warriors to call upon whatever resources they might need to resolve what looked to me like a hopeless situation in my life. I heard myself assigning these five warrior angels the formidable task of opening the minds of those who had become my enemies so that I might have the opportunity to at least present my equitable claims to them with their minds receptive to truth. After that request the warrior angels departed. They just disappeared from my sight. Slowly the immense light in the room faded to the softness of early dawn.

I was left with the assurance that, though I didn't know exactly how, the warrior angels would act. Several days passed. I was not terribly surprised when I received a telephone call from the president of the firm that had acquired my corporation. He was rude, but he did ask for a meeting with me two days before Christmas. The call was not friendly, but it was communication. I knew that the Warrior Angels were somehow mysteriously involved, but I didn't know in what way.

The president of the firm came to my office in Washington. He is a person who is always very much in control. He has a unique ability to manipulate every circumstance: He can be most charming or most difficult. His behavior depends upon the composition of the people he is dealing with. As he came into my office, we went through the formalities. Then he sat down.

The first thing I recognized was how extremely uncomfortable he was. As he sat in his chair fidgeting, the sun suddenly pierced the clouds of a dreary day and came streaming through the window right into his eyes. He winced. He squinted, moved first to one side, then to the other. He could not get a clear view of me. I had never seen this powerful man act in such a way before. His discomfort escalated. He wanted to be out of that room! We talked quickly about my understanding of his firm's liability for the acquisition of my corporation. With few words we came to an agreement that mirrored the terms we had agreed to seven months earlier. He verbally agreed to all the terms and promised to fax the corrected contract to me by five o'clock that day. He left my office with a warning: "If you fail to sign the agreement exactly as my attorney drafts it today, I'll see you next in a courtroom."

At four o'clock I received the promised fax. The wording was totally contrary to the discussion we had just completed. It was amazing; the document was worded as if we had never talked. It was totally unacceptable. It was not possible for me to reach him. I was faced with the five-o'clock deadline. Closing the door of my office, I got down on my knees and started to pray.

At ten minutes to five the man telephoned me from his car. I explained to him that I had much difficulty with the document. He exploded. He raged in a steady stream of expletives, then slammed down the phone. I thought, "It's all over!" Then I slumped into my chair and really began to pray as never before in my life. It was not a great prayer. It was the prayer of a broken man. I had come so close, then lost.

About a half hour later I was surprised to receive a phone call from his assistant informing me that he was unable to reach the firm's attorney. He said the attorney would be in touch with me the next day, Christmas Eve. At that point I knew the only choice I had was to trust the power of God. But my prayers became more hopeful! I didn't sleep much that night.

The next morning I received a fax from the firm's attorney. I read the document. Then I read it again. Not only did it contain all of our original terms agreed to seven months earlier, it included much more than I had asked for or expected. I was flabbergasted! Seven months of agony were instantly wiped away. I signed the document immediately and faxed it back with the words "Merry Christmas and Happy New Year" attached to the front.

How did such a dramatic reversal occur in only twenty-four hours with no human intervention? My warrior friends did their job extremely well.

Ben's story describes Angel Power at work in a very tangible way. When asked why he should merit such high-level intervention in his business crisis, Ben admitted:

That's a question I have struggled with for some time. I do not believe I am special, but I have always believed in the power of prayer. I have always believed that we do have Guardian Angels.

I see and speak to my own Guardian Angel all the time. I have done this since I was a small child. His name is Michael. He is not one of the Warrior Angels, though he knows them all and has the ability to summon them all at a moment's notice. Michael can be in many places at the same time. He is a philosopher, a political adviser, a statesman. He comes from the Choir of Angels that administrates countries. It is very clear to me that he has the characteristics of a statesman because we

have talked about it. He is someone who has access to vast resources. His intellect and knowledge are immeasurable.

I have never seen him with my eyes as I did the Warrior
Angels. Rather I see him in my mind's eye. Michael appears, in
terms of our age, perhaps mid-thirties. He is big, virile, with
curly blond hair. He wears white or sometimes blue robes.

One day Michael and I were talking in my car as I drove
to Pennsylvania. I was struggling with the issue of feeding the
world's hungry. This is an issue I care about greatly. He asked
me, "Where did Joan of Arc, a sixteen-year-old peasant girl,
get the knowledge, the strength, the wisdom she needed to
lead the French army to victory?"

On another day I was struggling with a grave concern,
a policy issue that involved many lives and much money.
Michael said "You don't need to talk to me about that. Speak
to the Blessed Mother. She is sitting in the backseat." I froze
momentarily. If Michael said she was in the backseat . . . she
was there! Michael has told me several times that I should talk
to the Blessed Mother directly.

I did not want to see the Blessed Mother. I had no idea
how to speak to her or what to say. Michael understood. He
told me that the best is yet to come. He said that those who
know the Blessed Mother well come closest to God in this life.
I am working to prepare myself spiritually to meet her. Michael

says she comes only where she is invited. He reminds me often that she is the Mother of Love, the Mother of humankind and the Queen of Angels. He says she has many gifts from God to give me. Michael wants me to have the gifts. He has told me that to obtain these gifts, I must ask the Blessed Mother. I am in the process of trying to address her. I have not yet been able to do so.

Angelic Deeds

Ben's story demonstrates the plight of a man who has lost all hope in a human solution to his immense loss. He had no other remedy but prayer as he faced his personal problems. In his time of great distress Ben learned that the holy angels have been given to us to be our protectors and our best and most effective friends. They have the power to make the paths of life easier for us by illumining them with the light of truth. The angels have clearer vision of truth than most humans. They know that the great God of Abraham called to each one of us before He made the world. When God called to us, we came forth out of His Heart overflowing with love. We are His Love. We need to love and be loved. Any other behavior destroys our life.

Ben admits that he knows his own Guardian Angel quite well. Yet he was amazed to discover how profoundly the angels desire to rescue us from fear, failure, isolation, and loneliness. Ben's story gives us a view of the powerful angels who are constantly available to help us access God's Kingdom of Love, where there is a plentitude of all the things our hearts most deeply crave. Angels remind those who respond to their gracious proddings that all pain and suffering are short-lived.

The Bible speaks of many persons who have learned, after the fact, that sin is the consequence of failure to obey God's Will. How do we recognize God's Will? Unfortunately, over the centuries people have used their own distorted perceptions of "God's Will" to wreak harm and havoc. Sick, would-be religious "martyrs" have been known to kill or maim people in a misguided personal mission to obtain entrance to Heaven for themselves. Other misguided people grab all the assets or power that their human strength permits in the name of God's Will, believing that might makes right. Still others lead lives of hopelessness and despair while blaming "God's Will" for their own weaknesses and mistakes. Many people with absolutely opposing viewpoints can and do claim to represent "God's Truth" or "God's Will" only as it aggrandizes their own appetites and desires, even at the expense of others, the planet, and the cosmos.

God wills peace, joy, abundance, and true love for each one of us. We are all His children. God created each of us, the earth, the cosmos, and the heavens. He loves what He creates. Those who realize this truth and live out the consequences of such knowledge experience joy at their being. They ponder well the words He has imparted; they embrace His doctrines with wonder and awe. They learn to live in God's Kingdom of Love. The journey is a process.

Angels empower God's children to see Him in the world. They communicate messages of His immense, unfathomable love for each child of His. Angels sing of God the Father of all the living, the source and goal of all life. God, who loves what He creates, loves His Dear children unconditionally. When His children call to Him, God responds. He sends angels to draw near with His Providence.

Angels always see the face of God. They mirror His Humility. They tirelessly bring His Love to His Precious children of the earth. The angels weep in agony for us when we run from God. They know how dangerous it is for us to abandon the protection of God's Ways. Angels, however, bow before the freedom God had given His children. We are all quite free to choose God or to deny Him. Angels recognize that when we refuse God's Love, we choose death. When all humankind recognizes this truth, the Kingdom of Heaven will fill the earth, for all will choose love. Love begets love. Love never dies. Love is eternal life.

The Bible teaches that God closed and guarded with a fiery sword the entrance to the Garden of Eden (Genesis 3:23–24). The earth became a valley of suffering when God's children no longer had access to the Garden of Eden. When we lost Paradise, we lost the ability to see Truth. The fiery sword that blocks the entrance to Paradise is the great sword of conscience. It takes awareness every minute to keep the sword of conscience on fire with the light of Truth. It is Angel Power that brings such awareness. Those who access Angel Power and are clothed with the holy angels are able to pass through the fiery sword of conscience to reenter Paradise.

The angels are exquisitely aware of God's Great, Unfathomable Love for each of us. They watch God's Will being communicated daily to His children. The angels know that it takes patience and charity to do God's Work. Angels are blessed spirits of pure patience. They are blessed spirits of pure, tested love. Love is blessed charity.

Angel Power helps us to grow in love. Real love is selfless love. It is steeped purely in Truth. Real love is possible only when we are surrendered to God's Will. Then we are able to love for God and through God and with God. Love for any other reason is selfish love, which has no lasting value. Selfish love blocks Angel Power.

The angels are selfless spirits who mediate the pure love of God to humankind. To love selflessly as angels do means to love God above all the things He has created, including ourselves. To love that way, we must know God well. Angels constantly labor to bring us to see the face of God at all times. Those who pray much know God.

Angel Power changes attitudes and behavior. Love for others, when there is no perceived gain, in the earthly sense, is everlasting treasure, and the angels know it. They tirelessly inspire us to motives for behavior toward one another that are higher than mere self-aggrandizement. The measure of our love for others is a test of our love for God. It is a sign of active Angel Power. Love does not die with the human body. Love lives on from generation to generation.

The angelic warriors who helped Ben no doubt were assigned to his situation because he prayed so fervently with deep, though painful, trust, and because his cause was just. They must have experienced much joy at being able to demonstrate God's Unfathomable Love for His children. The great Warrior Angels are assigned by God to come to the speedy rescue of all those who pray, trust, and struggle to live in justice, kindness, and integrity before the face of God on earth. Ben's story is everyone's possibility.

Meditation

ACCESS THE POWER OF MY ANGELS

My Enemy leads My children deep into the valley of worldly
  comforts, worldly prizes, worldly pleasures.
Then he corrupts My Harmony, My Peace.
Worldly pleasure taints the purity of My Image in your soul.
Worldly pleasure dims your eyes to My Presence in the world.
Worldly pleasure creates a din in your ears that silences My Voice.
Often in the silence of suffering you find My Heart.
Cling to the aloneness of suffering.
Know that the aloneness you feel is My Waiting Arms.
I am beyond the world. I am the whole world. I am your world.
I am your life. I am your hope.
I alone am Truth. I alone am Life.

Access the power of My Angels.

Prayer

Our Father Who art in Heaven, Hallowed be Thy Name.

Thy Kingdom come.

Thy will be done on earth as it is in Heaven.

Give us this day our daily bread.

Forgive us our trespasses as we forgive those who trespass
    against us.

Lead us not into temptation. Deliver us from all evil.

For Thine is the Kingdom, the power, and the glory forever.

Amen

Chapter Three

Angels of
Consolation

✦

Suddenly an angel of the Lord stood by him and a light shone in the
cell. He tapped Peter on the side and awakened him, saying, "Get
up quickly." The chains dropped from his wrists. The angel said to
him, "Put on your belt and your sandals." He did so. Then he said
to him, "Put on your cloak and follow me."

—ACTS 12:7–8

Angels comprehend that frequently there is a higher purpose to suffering than
the immediate pain and misery that preoccupy humans. Suffering is a powerful instrument that rips away illusion. Those who turn to a higher power in
the torment of suffering access angels of consolation, who draw near and
abide with them. No one can function in chaos. Angels of consolation lift

those who rely upon them out of chaos to the mountain of peace, where all the blessings of God await us. Those who find peace find solutions to all life's challenges.

Jennifer's Story

Jennifer had three children. The oldest was not yet four. The weather was bitter outside, and Jennifer was feeling close to despair. Her husband, a traveling sales-man, was asleep upstairs in the tiny house, and all the babies were asleep too.

Jennifer looked at the shabby kitchen heaped with dishes, pots and pans, and dirty laundry. On the table was the carcass of the smallest turkey she'd ever seen, left from Christmas dinner. Jim wasn't bringing much money home these days. She didn't know what he loved anymore, except his martinis. "O God, do you exist?" Jennifer cried as she wondered how she could go on.

The doorbell rang, and the baby began to cry at the same time. Who would come on this bitter Christmas night? Jennifer had no family in the big city of Chicago. It was probably dangerous to open the door. But the doorbell rang incessantly, and another baby was crying upstairs.

Quickly Jennifer opened the front door just a crack. A frail old woman in a threadbare coat smiled graciously at her. "My car broke down. Please may I use your phone?" she inquired quite sweetly. Realizing there was no danger and by now frantic at the sounds of children crying, Jennifer let the old woman in and showed her where the phone was as she raced up the stairs to tend to her children.

No more than five minutes later Jennifer came down the steps to look for the old woman. There was no one there. The kitchen was spotless. Every dish was washed, dried, and replaced in the cupboard. The laundry was clean, folded, and even ironed! All the worn undershirts and baby clothes were not only mended, they looked brand-new! The floors were shining, the windows sparkled, and the few items of furniture that Jennifer had received from her mother were glistening. Even the children's toys were neat. The discarded gift wrappings and rubbish were nowhere to be found.

Astounded, Jennifer opened the refrigerator. A golden turkey, freshly roasted and bulging with the chestnut stuffing her mother had always made, sat on the center shelf. And there were pies—apple and mince. Jennifer had not been able to afford pies, nor had she tasted any since her mother died three years earlier.

"Mom?!" Jennifer cried out.

Suddenly, in that moment of awareness, chains of hopelessness, fatigue, and fear fell from Jennifer. A surge of energy exhilarated her. She began to laugh at her own foolishness. It was certainly not "God's Will" that she live in squalor, poverty, and oppression! Now Jennifer knew it! Her own fear and weakness had nearly ruined her life and the life of her three children, who did not ask to be born. Jennifer recognized that the poor, frail old woman who came to her door that Christmas night could easily be a living replica of her own damaged self-image. The light of truth showed Jennifer the options that were available to her to correct the mistakes of her past. The desperate plea "God, do you exist?" had drawn His Angel of Mercy to Jennifer's misery.

The following afternoon Jennifer found a clergyman who was sympathetic to her problems. With the help of a caring congregation, Jennifer obtained assistance for her children, her own educational and employment needs, and Jim's addictions.

Thirty years later Jennifer and her husband are the grateful parents of three college-educated children. When Jim retired, the couple moved to Florida, where Jennifer owns and manages her own business. Both are active in the family outreach programs of their community.

Jennifer's journey out of despair began when she realized unequivocally that angels do exist, that they do care about all the details of our life, and that they have the power to help us acknowledge our inherent dignity, to change ourselves and the circumstances of our life. Jennifer's story is a pattern for all those who believe no one cares.

Any one angel is capable of remedying all the pain in the entire cosmos. Clothed in Angel Power, those who suffer enter a path of light, for angels are spirits of pure peace. Those who access Angel Power experience peace in the face of suffering. They are quite secure in God's Providential Care as His Glorious Angels comfort and inspire them. Angel Power produces abandonment to the will of God, which is pure human freedom.

It is never God's Will that His children live in bondage to people, places, or things. God requires us to acknowledge our dignity. God's Love for us is the essence of human dignity.

All suffering is not the same. The Twelve Step program of Alcoholics Anonymous offers versions of the following prayer, which has brought much light to people all over the world:

> *God grant me the serenity*
> *To accept the things I cannot change*
> *The courage to change the things I can,*
> *And the wisdom to know the difference.*

Those with incurable diseases and handicaps, or painful permanent relationships, or living in difficult, dangerous geographic regions from which they cannot escape, need all the Angel Power they can access to bear their affliction with dignity and peace. The ever-present angels are aware of the pain, distortion, and misery that attaches to regions, families, persons, and events.

No one escapes suffering. No one escapes death. Some people and even places seem to suffer more than others. Angels are God's Instrument of Consolation for those who call to Him.

Angel Power in Abandonment

An old woman lay crippled in her bed in a state-run nursing facility. No family remembered her. No one came to visit. Each day brought more desolation to her life. Turning in desperation to the memory of the angels of her childhood, the old woman wept bitterly. She dared to ask the angels why they had forgotten her. Her Guardian Angel immediately appeared to her in a glorious ray of celestial light. Later the old woman recalled that the dazzling angel bent over her bed and assured her with the following words:

> I watch over you. You are not alone. I bring your prayers bathed in tears of sorrow to the Throne of God. Angels are with you. We bring you strength to bear all that God allows in your life. You are shedding your attachments to the earth and the things of the earth, which are transistory. God calls His children to Himself. He frees them from their bondage. He brings them along the path of His Son Jesus to Himself. Each soul must pass through the valley of suffering to come to God's Waiting Arms. God's Love guides and comforts each of His children. Those who comfort the afflicted will be comforted. Through sufferings you learn to love God with all your heart. Keep up your courage.

On facing page: Nothing is impossible for those who pray and trust God's Promises.

After the old woman's visit with her Guardian Angel, others in the nursing home began to notice a sweet joy that seemed to envelop her. Her peaceful smile comforted all those who approached her. Soon the angels carried her to the Empyrean Valleys of Paradise.

Angel Power Is Dignity

Though not every suffering need be endured, as Jennifer learned, some types of suffering are inescapable. The old woman could not help herself physically. No loved ones came to comfort her. She prayed, in her great sorrow, and the angels of God's Mercy drew near to comfort her affliction. She accessed Angel Power. Much of the misery of the world can be eliminated by awakening to the availability of Angel Power in a cooperative venture with people of goodwill. When holy angels and humans work together for the glory of God, the portal of Heaven opens. All live in peace, dignity, and justice.

Angel Power, in concert with loving human commitment, rights wrongs, eliminates injustice, cures the sick, and manages the assets and liabilities of this imperfect world. Jennifer's family was a beneficiary of such enlightened understanding. The old woman's family was not. Both women were enabled by angels to acknowledge their own inherent dignity.

It takes strength, which angels bring; courage, which angels impart; and great wisdom to ascend to the interior mountain of tranquillity where dignity, peace, joy, and love are the reward for those who access and acquire Angel Power. Angel Power is the light of Truth. Angel Power is love in action.

Why don't angels intervene and eliminate suffering? Perhaps they do in ways of which we are as yet unaware. Angels can and want to do more for each of us. The choice is ours.

Humans sometimes become what they observe. The choice of how to respond to the issues and circumstances of each day belongs to each one of us personally. God is pure love. Those who choose to know God well learn to love. Those who love are conduits of love for others. Where there is love there is happiness, contentment, and abundance. Where there is love there is God.

Suffering ironically often frees God's Beloved children from those things and attitudes and attachments that cannot live in His Kingdom of Love. Angel Power is an exquisite antidote to the raw agony of human suffering. Angel Power is the power of love. The power of love heals all wounds.

Angels sometimes come when we least expect them, and often they are disguised in ways that allow us to admit them into our lives. They bring out the best in us when we cooperate with God's Will. They also bring rewards from the Heavenly City.

One of the great gifts angels bring to those who access Angel Power is the ability to meet nonlove with love. How? By the sweet cross of patience. Sometimes the person who requires the most patience from us is ourself. When we are patient, we forgive every injury and disappointment and personal failure through God and in God and with God. When we walk with God attired in

Angel Power, we begin to comprehend how all things are possible. It is God who carries our hurts. He carries our disappointments. He compensates for our limitations and mistakes.

Angel Power allows us to understand our choices. They do not die with our body. Our choices live on for all eternity. Our choices are the ladder to Paradise. With holy Angel Power we learn never to respond to any situation except with love. The following poem is a song of peace that accesses Angel Power:

SONG OF PEACE

Love comes from God.
Love leads to God.

Love is firm.
Love is gentle.

Love is always forgiving.
Love is always patient.
Love never tires.
Love never remembers nonlove.

Love comes from God.
Love leads to God.

Those who love have peace. Those who love are peace. In prayer we develop the strength to love. The more we pray, the more we are able to love. The more we love, the closer we are to God. God is love and it is His Love with which we love. God invites us to live forever in His Love.

Angel Power is a pure gift of God's Love. In prayer we access Angel Power. It is with the help of holy angels that we transcend the limitations of our human condition to fly on their wings into the very Heart of God. Every real treasure exists only in the Heart of God. God alone is Love.

We show our love for God by obedience to His Will. His Will is that we love one another as we love ourselves. In our disobedience we experience deformed, selfish love. Selfish love brings no peace. Selfish love brings no joy. The pleasure that comes from selfish love does not satisfy the cravings of the human heart. It is only in obedience to God's Will that we experience peace.

Love is charity. God demands that we grow in love. Love is possible only when we surrender to His Will. Then we are able to love for God, and through God, and with God. Love for any other reason is selfish love. Selfish love has no lasting value. Love for others, when there is no gain for us in the earthly sense, is everlasting treasure. Our love for others measures the depth of our love for God.

Authentic love is firm. Authentic love is never self-righteous. Authentic love is a servant as God is servant of all. His Angels are servants of humanity and of the cosmos too. Most people do not yet recognize God as servant. It takes humility to see God as servant. God alone is Humility. He is hidden everywhere. Angels, brilliantly humble, know Him. They are hidden everywhere too. They see God. They want us to see Him, too, for they know such is His Will for us. Angels tell us in countless ways of the Humility of God. Angels mirror the Humility of God. Angels constantly invite us to mirror the Humility of God too.

Those who access Angel Power experience God serving as sunshine to warm us. Those who access Angel Power recognize God as the great vine grower, supplying us with sweet grapes that become the wine to warm our hearts. Those who access Angel Power see God's Smiling Face in the crystal-clear lake that bears the fishes to feed our nations. Those who access Angel Power understand that God is fashioning answers to the disease, pollution, and war that plague the nations of the earth as He knits each tiny baby in the womb of a cooperating mother.

God alone is Truth. God is Spirit. He lives in the heart of all creation. We live in His World. His is the Kingdom and the Power and the Glory.

The angels are purveyors of God's Grace. Angels are eternal spirits of peace, joy, and everlasting love. They dwell in Heaven and on earth too. They never get old. They never get sick. They do not die. Angels are always perfectly good and exquisitely beautiful.

Angels personally and individually watch over us. They love us with God's Infinite Love. They love us unfathomably more than we love ourselves or one another. The angels always see Truth. They want us to see Truth too.

Angels are created by God. So also are we. Angels are not, nor have they ever been, mortals. They have never had human bodies. Humans, however, can be angels when they are messengers or instruments of God's Love. In the Divine Vision, humans are called by God to be angels of His Love and Mercy to one another. Such behavior brings the Kingdom of Heaven on earth.

Angels profoundly desire to help us ascend the mountain of love as they watch over us. They invite us to share every part of our lives with them. They long for us to be perfectly happy, as they are. Angels are always gracious. They never interfere with our freedom of choice. Angels actively help us, though we are mostly unaware of their presence.

Each angel is unique and different from the others, just as each person is unique and different from all other people in the world. Each has special powers and gifts. There is no other person like you or me, nor will there ever be. Each of us is a masterpiece of God's creation, designed, created, and loved by Him from all eternity. So also is each angel a masterpiece of God's Love.

There are legions of powerful angels who are assigned to help us, please us, surprise us, enlighten us. At God's Bidding, angels continuously create the environments for us to dwell in the light and splendor of God as they do.

God is undisturbed Serenity. Those who know God experience peace, joy, and love. Their life is abundance. Angels are messengers, guides, and protectors, given to each of us by God during our time on the earth. Their mission is to support gracious life for those who choose to access their power.

Many people throughout history have spoken through art, literature, and music of the beautiful angels they have seen in their dreams. They cherish the expectation of the rustle of angel wings on a bright, warm day, and the lilt of angel voices wherever love reigns. We are called to no less.

An angel of the Lord is standing nearby. The light of Truth shines all about. Will you notice as the angel of the Lord taps you? Your own angel is calling, "Wake up! Hurry, get up! Put on your cloak and follow me!" The "cloak" is the cloak of Truth.

Meditation

I am Love.

Love comes from Me.

Drink of the fountain of My Love.

Love is patient. Love is long-suffering.

When you grow weary, think of Me.

Think of My Patience with you.

Think of Me always. Then you will become like Me.

Imitate Me in every second of your life.

See My Face. Look at My Endurance.

All My Suffering was My Gift to you.

*When you see My Suffering, you see gentle acceptance of the
    human condition.*

You are My Redeemed children. Live like redeemed children.

*I came into the world to save you from the very things you continue
    to focus on.*

Look to Heaven. Concentrate on the work of the Kingdom.

Choose the Garden of Paradise.

Access the Power of My Angels.

Prayer

God our Father,

You are the Lord of Love and Mercy.

Place Your Kindness in us.

Change our hearts into vessels of Your Love.

Send Your Mighty Angels of Peace

To enlighten and console us

Along every step of our

Journey to Your Waiting Arms.

Amen

On facing page: For God commands the angels to guard you in all your ways. With their hands they shall support you lest you strike your foot against a stone. —Psalms 91:11–12

Chapter Four

Angel Power
in the World

✦

For God commands the angels
to guard you in all your ways.
—PSALMS 91:11

Everyone knows about the great cosmic laws God has given to us for our safety and protection. They are written upon each human heart. Those who choose to obey are the ones who love God and enjoy Angel Power. Obedience to God's Laws is a sign of love and trust. It is a freely chosen act rooted in Truth.

Angels have exquisite minds, far superior to our minds. Their reservoir of knowledge includes not only the entire universe but the secrets of Heaven too. We humans:

stand behind the wall of our body, sheltered from strangers' eyes in the hidden recesses of our mind; and when we wish to, we step forth through the gateway of language to show ourselves as we are within. But angels have only the first barricade, and as soon as one of them wants to make known his thoughts, they are made known.[1]

Angels are capable of seeing the past, the present, and the future all at once. Normally we only see one image at a time. Angels are able to see much more clearly than we the consequences of each word and deed of ours. Our vision is not that keen. Our wisdom is not that astute. For those reasons alone all people need Angel Power if the sting of human suffering is to be conquered. The angels always warn us when our actions are harmful. They know what is best for us, what will bring us the most happiness. Angels have the power to change what needs to be changed, to protect what needs to be protected, and to fix whatever needs to be fixed. God has given them authority to make our lives happy, prosperous, fulfilled, and joyous. Except in specific circumstances, angels are powerless to act on our behalf unless we consciously access their power.

A colleague was leaving on the noon flight for Europe. It was 10:30 A.M. and there were many details to attend to both at work and at home. Suddenly he realized that he had left a critical textbook in a building in the city, thirty miles away. There was no time to go to the city to get the book or to have it delivered to the airport.

The sacred texts assure us that angels are quite willing to help us in our need. He quickly prayed. The book definitely would be used to help others, as well as himself. He felt some confidence creep into his prayer as he asked God to send an angel to get the book and place it on the hall table beside his briefcase.

Somewhat embarrassed by his prayer to cover for his own negligence, he felt doubt flood his mind. "Who do I think I am that an angel should solve my problem?" he said to himself. He quickly checked himself: "Do I believe in the presence and power of the angels or not?" He sighed at his weak faith and prayed: "Lord, You are the King of the angels, the Lord of my life and the protector of my weaknesses. I trust Your Love and Your Power. Please grant Your Angels permission to deliver the textbook I so urgently need." He quietly mentioned to his astonished assistant, "I believe the angels are placing that textbook on the hall table right now. It is there beside my briefcase." "Sure, good luck" was the faint response.

He refused to give in again to the temptation to doubt the angels' help. Though he did not know exactly why, he recognized that to doubt was to curtail the power of angels to help him. Several people, aware of the dilemma, knew exactly where the book was located back in the city. Some tension developed as word of the angelic request filtered around.

When he walked into the hall, the textbook was there on the table beside his briefcase! He laughed with such joy that everyone came rushing to the hall. Amazement filled the office with a stunned silence.

The sweet virtues of humility, trust, and obedience to the will of God are the halcyon bulwark of Angel Power. Saint Michael the Archangel is the di-

vinely appointed champion and warrior captain of the Angel Forces of Divine Tranquillity.[2] He is the patron of humility and obedience. This great Archangel is also the patron and protector of the humble who actively seek to obey the will of God in their lives. Saint Michael the Archangel is the banner of Truth.

Angel Power Under the Ground

At the southernmost tip of Italy, in the kingdom of Naples in the year 490, a tired old bull became trapped in a cave on Mount Gargano. The heartrending cries of the frightened animal induced the owner to bring out his bow. He shot an arrow at the bull to kill it. Legend has it that the arrow changed course and turned instead on the archer. The locals were afraid. The arrow incident indicated that the natural law was reversed. Why? "What was God trying to tell us?" they asked themselves. They summoned the Bishop, Saint Lawrence. He had no answer. More insight was needed, so he declared a three-day prayer-and-fast vigil at the entrance to the cave. All the people prayed that they might understand God's Will. Their obedience, prayer, and fasting accessed Angel Power in a dramatic way. During the prayer vigil Saint Michael the Archangel appeared to the Bishop, announcing:

On facing page: Saint Michael the Archangel is the Warrior Champion of God's Will. Angels personally intervene in crises to protect families, nations, cities, airports, buildings, churches, houses, and vehicles.

I am the Archangel Michael, who is always in the presence of the Lord. I have been sent in response to the faithful, who are gathered here in this cave in obedience, prayer, and humility. This cave has been chosen as a place to illumine the faithful with the Light of the Unseen God.

Henceforth this place shall be considered sacred. Teach the people that it is not by the blood of animals that sin is forgiven. It is the blood of the Lord Jesus Christ that washes away sin. All that is sincerely asked in prayer and fasting in this place will be granted.[3]

Three years later, on May 8, 493, Saint Michael the Archangel appeared once again to inform the Bishop, Saint Lawrence, that the ground under the cave was consecrated by angels. When the Bishop announced the apparition and message of Saint Michael the Archangel, all were in awe. After three days of prayer and fasting certain people were selected to break through the underground cave. There they found a magnificent subterranean church hollowed out of the solid rock! Soon pilgrims to Saint Michael's Cave noticed a liquid substance dripping from the ceiling. Those whom it touched were quickly healed of their maladies. Word spread like fire throughout Christendom of the miraculous underground church hewn out of the rocks by Saint Michael and the angels on Mount Gargano. People flocked to the incredible underground church from everywhere. Devotion to the angels flourished.

Pope Boniface quickly began construction of the Michelon Basilica on Mount Circo along the Salarian Way in Rome. When the basilica was completed, it was consecrated to Saint Michael the Archangel, and the universal church established his special feast day as September 29th.

The cave of Saint Michael the Archangel is considered a holy place even in modern times. People of all faiths journey there to access Angel Power, hoping to receive favors from the Prince of the Angelic Court and the angels. It is believed that throughout the centuries no one has ever been disappointed.

Perhaps the tired old bull is a symbol of tired old humanity. Do we weep and mourn and cry at the door of Paradise? The arrow that would silence us is God's Love for us that has pierced His Own Heart. He constantly pours His Love for us into the world. Countless millions of His Angels are continuously dispatched to assist, guide, and protect us as we grow fully in the wonderful, harmonious image and likeness of God in which He created us. The angels have been busy at this job since the beginning of humankind.

The angels love us with God's Love. That love is totally pure. They desire that we share the beautiful vision of God they continuously enjoy. The angels want us to access Angel Power for the glory of God. They know we are His Hope and His Glory.

Angel Power in the Air

At the end of the sixth century, under the papacy of Saint Gregory the Great, an infestation of the dreaded plague was brutally eradicating the population of Rome. The Holy Father carried a statue of the Blessed Mother, under her title Queen of the Angels, through the streets of Rome, imploring the help of God.

Legend says he asked for and received a miracle to end the plague in Rome. As he passed the old fortress of the Emperor Hadrian, great choirs of angels were heard filling the air with beautiful hymns of praise. Suddenly above the ancient rocks of the fortress could be seen a shining figure of a huge angel dressed in glistening armor. Raising his sword toward the sky, the angel was heard to announce:

I am the Archangel Michael, who always stands before the Throne of the Most High God.
Your prayers have been answered this day through the intercession of our Queen, the Blessed Virgin Mary.

As the powerful Archangel thrust his sword back into its scabbard, great flashes of light radiated throughout the sky. Colors of such beauty that few could describe their glory were seen by all. Local lore speaks of the plague that ceased that day. It is said that no further cases were diagnosed. In gratitude the fortress was renamed the Castle San Angelo (the Castle of the Holy Angel), and a magnificent statue of Saint Michael the Archangel was placed atop the site to remind the people of the miracle.

Angels do wonderful things. They are not gods. They are not divine. They themselves do not work miracles. They bring miracles. All miraculous power belongs to God alone. Angels are agents of God. It is His Will that angels guard, guide, and serve the people of the earth, both for His Glory and for our peace, joy, and love.

Angel Power in the Water

In 1531 the Blessed Mother appeared in the New World at Guadeloupe, near Mexico City, to Juan Diego. Today the site is one of the most revered and venerated shrines in the world. Ten years later, in 1541, the Blessed Mother appeared once again, this time in Tlaxcala, to Native American Juan Diego Bernardino. She revealed a miraculous spring located in a glen of oak trees that flows freely even in these times. In addition to dramatic physical healings that were occasioned by drinking the flowing spring waters, a most unusual sign was given to validate the supernatural nature of the spring. The trunk of one of the oak trees bears the burnt image of the Blessed Mother.

Pilgrims bring the healing waters from the spring to their homes all over the world. A great basilica was constructed to honor the Blessed Mother's apparition and gift of the healing waters. It is called Our Lady of Ocotlan, which means, Our Lady of the Oak That Burned.

In 1631, the province of Tlaxcala once again received heavenly favors. A young Indian boy, Diego Lazaro, encountered Saint Michael the Archangel by interior illumination, as he participated in a religious procession in his small town of San Barnabe, twenty kilometers west of the capital city of Tlaxcala. On April 25, the Prince of the Heavenly Host spoke to the young man.

> *Know my son, that I am St. Michael, the Archangel. I come to tell you that it is God's will and mine that you tell the neighbors of this village and of its surroundings that in a ravine, which is made of two hills and is in front of this place, can be found a spring of miraculous water for all infirmities. It is under a big boulder.*
> *Don't doubt what I tell you, nor put aside what I command you.*[4]

Diego Lazaro disregarded the message. Unable to comprehend why someone of his lowly stature should be favored with a commission from the great Saint Michael the Archangel, he doubted the authenticity of his vision. He was unable to recognize his own dignity. His self-doubt led him to disobey the great Warrior Archangel. Quite suddenly Diego Lazaro fell mortally ill.

> Thirteen days after Saint Michael's first appearance and message [by interior illumination], on May 8 of that year, an "electrify-

ing" event occurred. The apparition that then took place, which is approved by the Church, is considered by some to be the greatest recorded and approved apparition of Saint Michael. . . . In one sudden, violent and terrifying instant, it looked like a bolt of lightning had crashed through the windows [of Diego Lazaro's home]. The mighty Archangel Saint Michael had entered and his manner of entrance frightened all others away.

In the presence of the great Prince of the Heavenly Host, Diego Lazaro was immediately healed of his mortal illness. The Archangel then transported Diego Lazaro to the ravine he had previously disclosed to him.

Here, where I touch with my staff, is the fountain that I spoke of. . . . You must make it known, or you will be gravely punished.

When Saint Michael the Archangel touched his sword to the ravine, immense flashes of light struck the earth, and bubbling waters came gushing forth. The great Archangel's voice echoed throughout the ravine:

"The light which you have seen descend from heaven is the virtue which God is giving to this spring for the health and healing of all infirmities and necessities. Make it known to all."

Struck with awe and holy zeal, Diego Lazaro never wavered until he found the healing spring that was shown to him by the Great Archangel. Then he once again lapsed into indifference.

Angels do have the authority to chastise us in order to force us to look at truth. Six months later Diego Lazaro was mysteriously struck with a mortal illness. This time he experienced excruciating pain. He had no idea that his disobedience to the Archangel might be influencing his physical condition. It is certain that each Guardian Angel constantly tries to communicate with his beloved human, even in ways of which we are not yet aware.

Writhing on his bed of agony, on November 13, 1531, Diego Lazaro became aware that Saint Michael the Archangel was towering over him.

The Archangel spoke:

"Why are you a coward and negligent in fulfilling what I entrusted to you?"

At once Diego Lazaro realized that he had not prayed for the strength and the courage to obey the commands of Saint Michael the Archangel. He had clung to the comfortable mediocrity of his life prior to his first apparition. He had failed to access Angel Power, which is the mediated power of Almighty God. Everyone on earth needs the strength and the courage to obey God's Will each day. Such strength is the fruit of prayer and fasting.

Looking up at the Archangel Michael, who is known as the Angel of Peace, Diego Lazaro heard the gracious voice of the Prince of the Heavenly Host:

Get up and make known what I have commanded you.

Diego Lazaro was of course healed of all his infirmities. He journeyed at once to the Bishop, Guttierre Bernardo Quiroz, who agreed to have the waters of the spring investigated. "All who drank the water regained perfect health." The Church, after three scrutinizing investigations, pronounced the miraculous nature of the spring and the authenticity of the three apparitions of Saint Michael the Archangel. Diego Lazaro had finally shed the garments of selfishness. He spent the rest of his life at the spring serving the sick and the poor who came there to seek the mercy of God.

Today a magnificent basilica, San Miguel del Milagro, welcomes pilgrims from all over the world who come to the healing waters. Through the centuries those who have treated the waters irreverently have brought upon themselves various problems similar to those Diego Lazaro encountered when he responded irreverently to the call of the warrior Archangel Michael.

It is not yet understood why, but the spring, which had become dry many years before, suddenly started producing miraculous waters again in 1984. The waters flowed freely until 1989. Then, for no apparent reason, they dried up. On July 28, 1990, the miraculous waters once again began to flow freely at San Miguel del Milagro.[5]

The shrine is located two hours southeast of Mexico City. Angel Power is infused into the waters of the spring and the faithful come from all over the world to drink. Miraculous healings continue to be reported at San Miguel del Milagro.

Angel Power Destroys Negativity

Angels are administrators of God's Mercy. It is a sad fact of the human journey on earth that those who dwell on mistakes in themselves or others reactualize the mistakes and give them power to enslave. Those who choose to ascend the spiritual mountain of enlightenment quickly surrender mistakes, failures, and inadequacies to God's Mercy. Angels guide people who respond to their presence to move beyond personal human suffering and limitations. They help to guard the contents of human consciousness.

Negative thoughts, feelings, and emotions beget nontruth and produce illusion. Those who dwell on negative thoughts give them life. However, pretending dark thoughts do not exist does not make them go away. Juan Bernardino succumbed to his negative thoughts and emotions. Perhaps he did not recognize them, and therefore could not rise above them. Saint Michael the Archangel acted most powerfully upon Juan's negativity. He awakened him by continued dramatic appearances, warnings, including sickness, and rewards that the sacred waters produced.

The Angel Power that Juan Bernardino received is the heritage of all the children of angels. God created no one to languish in pain, sorrow, and hopelessness. The work of the holy angels is to lift God's People to the heights of His Glory. Those who entertain negative thoughts and emotions, as Juan Bernardino did when he refused to believe the wonderful messages and appearances of the great Saint Michael the Archangel, risk *becoming* the negative emotions. Even to speak a negative word is to curse ourselves. Such words act as a boomerang. He or she who curses becomes the curse.

Angels are busy remedying all the negativity in the world. Those who access Angel Power ascend upon the wings of the angels to the sweet, pure winds of God's Love and Providence.

It is God's Will that angels have the power and the authority to bless and correct any mistakes of action or judgment that befall a human. It takes awareness of the danger of negative thinking to overcome its cunning. A humble person will accept correction from a trusted confidant. Angels will not interfere in our journey unless we choose to include them in the process of our life. If we invite angels to enlighten our judgment, they warn us when we peer into the abyss of negativity.

Juan Bernardino fell into serious negativity based on his poor self-image, coupled with ignorance about the power and role of angels in the lives of human beings. His poor self-image was rooted in his ignorance about his relationship to God. He did not realize that he was God's Child, God's Treasure, God's Love. Saint Michael the Archangel showed him, and through the blessed, healing waters of San Miguel del Milagro, which flow even now, the great Archangel continues to show all of us who we really are. Each of us is God's Treasure. Many people, all over the world, sadly remain ignorant of their true relationship to God, even in these times.

The healing waters that flow in Mexico could be considered a sign of the clarity and sparkle of correct thinking. We become what we choose. True detachment illuminates the truth that the only chains are those we fasten upon ourselves. The immutable system of justice grinds on from generation to generation. We live out what we choose to think, to observe, and to do. Juan had three dramatic encounters with Saint Michael the Archangel that changed his life. Each of us has had many encounters with angels too. There will be more. The Era of Angels is upon us.

The earth is our temporary home, but it is not the home of angels. They realize that we dwell on the earth for a small amount of time. Angels are aware that God has endowed each person with the potential for a magnificent eternal destiny beginning right now. Though most of us spend less than one hundred years on the earth, we are destined to live eternally, based on the choices we make while we dwell on the earth. Angels live now in eternity. They are not bound by space and time as we are. Those who access their power develop the capacity to see the eternal value of each decision we make on earth.

Quite normal people from every continent and of every belief see or hear angels in these times. Most people in the quiet of their longings have experienced the presence and the wonder of God's Love, however fleeting the moment. The experience is so sweet that nothing assuages the desire for God. There are no atheists. Those who claim to be unbelievers have not yet tasted the Divine. It is to them in a most special way that God offers tender gentleness and legions of faithful angels in the dark night of doubt.

The truth is that God always sees us. He looks at us day and night. He constantly nurtures and sustains His Creation and His Creatures. The air we breathe, the sun that warms our faces, the water that quenches our thirst are

His Gifts to His Precious children. It is the awareness of His Eternal Presence in and about all that lives that brings peace, joy, and love.

Much of humanity is enchanted, unaware of God's presence. The angels, who are heralds of God's Glory, are busy awakening people to Truth all over the earth, now.

Meditation

Accept My Love.

To accept My Love you must accept My Resignation at the human
failings all around you.

Don't seek love and affirmation from creatures.

Seek from Me only. I am enough for you.

Give My Love to others. Give and give and give.

Come to Me when you are tired.

Come to Me when you feel the need for human love.

You can always find Me in the less fortunate.

I am hidden there waiting to love you and affirm you as you relieve
My Misery.

I left My Blessing on those who crucified Me so that It would come
back to you when you are scorned and mocked.

Be like Me.

Rejoice in My Love.

Only bless My Creation. Then you will be blessed.

Prayer

Saint Michael the Archangel,

Powerful Spirit of Truth.

Take my hand and lead me to Divine Truth.

Protect me from all the evil in the world.

Guard me and compensate for all my weaknesses.

Change, bless, and restore the consequences of all my mistakes.

Carry me on the wings of your love and might to the

Throne of God and pray to Him with me forever.

Amen

Chapter Five

Angel Power
in Others

✥

*The Son of Man did not come to be served but to serve and to give
his life as a ransom for many.*

—MATTHEW 20:28

The goal of Angel Power is to lift us into a reciprocity of love between one another. That love restores to us the Kingdom of Love. By serving others we
serve God, for He dwells in the least and in the mightiest. He is hidden in
others, waiting to affirm us as we relieve their misery.

The Story of Saint Catherine Labourè[1]

Paris is known as the City of Light and is considered by many to be the repository of great graces from Heaven. A seat of intellectual giants, it is a city where the arts, literature, industry, and geopolitics have flourished. Because of its past, however, it is sometimes referred to as Sin City.

Violence and turmoil came to Paris during the French Revolution, when the innocent and the guilty alike watered the earth with their blood. Good and evil live side by side in the world.

Women of all ages gathered at 140 Rue du Bac with a life commitment to serving the poor, educating the disadvantaged, and caring for the sick. They became known as the Sisters of Charity. Today their members serve the sick, the poor, and the disadvantaged everywhere.

Young Catherine Labourè aspired from early childhood to serve the lowly and less fortunate. She came to live at 140 Rue du Bac hoping to bring joy and help to those who believed no one cared for them.

It is said that on July 18, 1830, Catherine was awakened from sleep by a dazzling angel, who tapped her shoulder and said, "Catherine, come quickly. The Queen of Angels has been sent to this place with a great gift from God for all His People. She awaits you in the chapel with her Celestial Court."

Shocked, filled with awe, and somewhat frightened, Catherine responded to the angel, "If I get out of my bed to go to the chapel, I shall awaken the others." But the angel insisted, "Do not tarry!"

Dressing quickly, Catherine accompanied the brilliant angel. She wasn't certain that her feet ever touched the ground as she rushed through the convent to the chapel. With the angel at her side Catherine entered the chapel. Though it was the middle of the night, the chapel was ablaze with light.

The angel directed Catherine's gaze toward a chair upon the altar. By now the light was almost blinding as it radiated from the angels who surrounded the splendor of the Blessed Virgin Mary seated in the chair. The divinely beautiful Queen of Angels, an icon of tenderness, spoke these words:

I am the Blessed Mother of all God's children.
God hears the cries of His children.
I come to you as the Queen of Angels to bring God's Love
    to all in a special way.
The times are evil.
Great darkness has entered into the heart of humankind.
Do not be afraid.
God loves all His children with unfathomable love.
God has chosen you to be His Instrument in the world.
If you accept His Will, you must faithfully give the
    messages I confide to you to this unbelieving world.
You will be contradicted.
You will have much suffering, but you will have the grace
    to bear everything.
Much will happen in your lifetime.
Misfortunes will fall upon France.

The kingdom will fall.

Many will be severely persecuted.

Evil will spread to the whole world as the spirit of
rebellion is unleashed.

Those who pray receive great graces.

All prayer has value.

It is prayer that opens your eyes to see God in the world.

It is prayer that opens your ears to hear God in the world.

It is prayer that brings you into the Kingdom of Heaven.[2]

After this visitation Catherine devoted herself to prayer. As the weeks turned into months, Catherine looked for the Queen of Angels and her Celestial Court every time she entered the chapel. Something mysterious and inexplicable had happened to her that extraordinary night when the angel summoned her from sleep. She now felt a spiritual wound so deep that no human consolation could heal her. She retreated deeper and deeper into intense prayer, seeking the continuous conscious awareness of the presence of God in all that lives. She was being prepared for a great spiritual mission for the entire world. Her prayer was answered. Catherine now often dwelled in that world where God and she were one.

Early one morning, as Catherine knelt in the chapel, her eyes were once again suddenly opened to the presence of the Queen of Angels, who was standing upon a globe bathed in the brilliant and mysterious light of all angels. The light was so resplendent that the beatific Queen actually seemed "clothed with the sun." (Revelation 12). She wore rings on each of her fingers, and when she opened the palms of her hands, blazing rays of fire leaped forth to ignite the globe. The angels radiated immense, pulsating profusions of light as their Queen spoke the following words:

> *The ball that you see represents the planet Earth.*
> *These rays that shine from my hands symbolize the graces*
> *God has entrusted to me to give to those of His*
> *children who ask me for them.*
> *The gems from which rays do not shine are the graces for*
> *which my children forget to ask.*
> *The light of the angels symbolizes their power and presence*
> *on the earth.*
> *Allow me to help you, my children.*
> *Seek the light of the angels.*

The vision was more intense now. The rays from the outstretched hands of the Queen of Angels ignited fire upon all parts of the globe. A great golden door formed in an oval shape around the vision, the door to the Kingdom of Heaven.

The Queen of Angels spoke again:

> *It is God's Will that a medal be made bearing the image*
> *of this heavenly vision He has granted you.*
> *The medal will always be a sign of my protection and the*
> *presence of the angels to carry you along the paths of*
> *God's Unconditional Love for you.*

***All those who wear this medal with confidence will have
great graces, blessings, and strength.***

The medal was produced and distributed all over the world. Those who
wore the medal were so singularly blessed with miracles and divine favors that
it became known as the Miraculous Medal. Today, more than 150 years later,
people of all faiths, beliefs, races, and nationalities continue to wear the Miraculous Medal, for it has indeed proved to be a sign of Angel Power.

As a Sister of Charity, Catherine Labourè took the vows of poverty,
chastity, and obedience to acknowledge the dignity of the poor. She spent her
life in humble obscurity as a dedicated servant of the less fortunate at 140 Rue
du Bac. No one but her spiritual director was aware of Catherine's mysterious
and powerful experiences with the Queen of Angels and her Celestial Court
until after her death. Her spiritual director supervised the task of producing and
distributing the Miraculous Medal.

It is now known how frequently Catherine consciously experienced the
presence of the Living God during her life on earth. The modern world, however, has been bequeathed a miracle that speaks of the power of dwelling with
the angels in God's Kingdom of Love on earth.

Today the body of Saint Catherine Labourè rests in a glass casket in the
very chapel where her heavenly visitations occurred. More than 150 years have
passed, yet people still come from all over the world to view this ongoing miracle. As they draw near the exquisite beauty of the Saint's incorrupt remains,
many perceive that they have entered into a sacred chamber guarded by angels.

Angel Power Empowers

The more the presence of angels dawns upon the consciousness of humankind, the more the power of angels floods the earth with the light of God's
Love and His Confidence in us to make good choices. When Saint Catherine
Labourè awakened to the presence of the angel who tapped her shoulder, she
overcame her normal human incredulity and fear enough to get out of bed and
follow the angel. She persevered in her decision to pray and to serve the less
fortunate. She did not look for human consolations and prizes.

Angels empower us to love perfectly, as they do, for they are ministers of the
infinite love of God, which is ever unchanging. Angel inspirations, rooted in the
higher knowledge angels possess, help us to discern and obey God's Will. Angels
communicate the awareness to us that to recognize and obey God's Will is to love
perfectly. To love perfectly is to be totally loved. Love begets love.

Those who know holy angels well recognize and make God's Will their own.
In that way they dwell in the mansions of Paradise even while on earth, as Catherine
Labourè discovered. Her job, in the eyes of the world, was lowly. Her happiness
was unparalleled when she enjoyed the constant wonder of God's Presence.

It is not what we do for a living that matters. The real test of human hap-
piness is how faithfully we respond to what God has created us to do and to be.
When we discover who we really are, we tap the Divine Wellspring of God's
Love that empowers us to live in harmony with God's Great Plan for each of
His children. He made us to experience His Love, and to love not just in word
or speech but in our deeds and in truth.

A difficult obstacle in the human journey to Paradise is the pernicious disease of self-righteousness that attacks the unsuspecting. Angel Power is an effective remedy. A consequence of hidden pride, self-righteousness is a dark, deep closet in which garments of self-destruction are kept. Such garments are pulled out and worn as armor against imaginary enemies. Some never set aside their armor in this lifetime. The scribes and Pharisees Jesus confronted knew about self-righteousness. They were shocked at the friends and associates that Jesus chose. Jesus loved and served all. No one was excluded. He instructed His Followers to do the same.

It is sometimes said in fashionable (and not-so-fashionable) circles that "just because the Bible requires us to love someone doesn't mean we have to like that person." Such unenlightened thinking is the result of putting our own desires ahead of God's Will.

Angels are aware that every person is accompanied by a personal Guardian Angel. To dislike or refuse to love and serve anyone is to dislike and refuse to love and serve that person's Guardian Angel. To dishonor the angel is to dishonor God. Is not everyone on the earth a child of God our Father? They who choose not to like someone indulge in a negative fantasy steeped in pride. To love is to like. To like is to love. The motive for such a choice is obedience to the will of God.

The fastest road to spiritual enlightenment is to choose to like, love, and serve those who are difficult or distasteful, not for personal pleasure but for the love of God and His Holy Will. In that way the illusion of human power and control is put to death. Mastery over negative emotions is achieved. The need to control and manipulate is overcome.

Angels, who accompany us during our journey on earth, have the power to influence not only our perceptions but also those of others in our family, office, factory, bureau, or school. Angel Power can accomplish many of the goals that humans strut and fret, often in vain, to accomplish. Angels provide inspirations that give light and protection to circumstances and events. Angels have the power and the authority to bless and correct mistakes of action or judgment.

Saint Francis of Sales, a Bishop, founder of the Visitation Order, and Doctor of the Church, had great devotion to angels. He was a brilliant preacher whose words, it is said, brought healing to the hardest of hearts. He assured people of every background, belief, and nationality that God totally loves every human heart and burns with the desire to be loved in return, by humanity loving one another.[3] Some say Francis had the ability to see people's Guardian Angels. Before commencing a meeting, a sermon, a diplomatic encounter, before meeting a prince or a beggar, he would look intently at the person or audience. Francis of Sales admitted that he was asking the angels of those he encountered to dispose them to receive his words favorably, to inspire them with the powerful light of God, and to open their intellects to receive truth. He taught that those who ask shall receive. As a statesman Francis of Sales encouraged everyone to address the Guardian Angels of their enemies through prayer. Those who did so were spared any harm.[4] Such truth is a legacy for everyone.

The radiance of even one angel lights the entire earth (Revelation 18:1). Each person has a Guardian Angel, who radiates the intense light energy of God and bears within its essence His Infinite Power and Majesty. The precious gift of Angel Power brings the possibility for healing, mercy, compassion, graciousness, and familial unity to all people. Those who ask for it shall receive it.

Meditation

I AM WHO AM.

I AM THE SERVANT.

Though I am Power and Might, you find Me in littleness.

I am the servant of My Creature Man.
When man serves Me, he is one with Me.

When man serves himself, he cannibalizes My Creation.
He grows sick on the poison of selfishness and dies.

When you serve one another as I serve you, you are one with Me.

Those who live before My Face experience My Joy, My Peace.

Those who live in My Presence do only My Will.

Those who do only My Will have Heaven on earth.

I invite you to be a fellow servant with Me.
I AM WHO AM.

Prayer to Our Guardian Angel

Guardian Angel of mine
Assigned to me by God alone
Fashion in me a will like thine.

Strengthen me to obey all God's rules.
Strengthen me to cherish all God's promises.
Strengthen me to avoid all life's deceptions.
Strengthen me to accept all life's surprises.

Guardian Angel of mine
Chosen for me by God alone
Fashion in me knowledge like thine.

Guide me to seek the great truths.
Guide me to learn the great truths.
Guide me to treasure the great truths.
Guide me to dwell forever in the Great Truth. Amen

Chapter Six

Guardian Angels

Stricken with fear, the two men fell to the ground. But [Saint] Raphael [the Archangel] said to them: "No need to fear; you are safe. Thank God now and forever. As for me, when I came to you it was not out of any favor on my part, but because it was God's will. So continue to thank him every day; praise him with song.

—TOBIT 12:16–18

God's Divine Plan for His children of the earth includes His personal assignment of at least one special Guardian Angel to each of His children. A Guardian Angel can come from any of the Nine Choirs of Holy Angels. All the angels of all the Nine Choirs communicate with one another directly. An inferior angel can communicate with a superior angel at any time by directing pure thought toward that higher spirit. In this way any angel is able to access any other angel among the countless angels.[1] Humans are able to communicate with angels in the same way: by directing their thoughts toward all the angels, or toward specific Choirs, or toward particular angels, such as the Guardian Angel of a person, place, or thing.

Guardian Angels and their colleagues appear to us when and how we need them. They never come just to entertain us, distract us, or satisfy idle curiosity. Some Guardian Angels are quite active and filled with energy. Their presence is not difficult to detect. Some Guardian Angels are exceedingly mild. These angels usually guard those who are called to suffer much.

The diaries of German mystic Mechtilde, known as the Ancilla Domini, who died in 1919, are widely circulated because she described a visual relationship with her Guardian Angel and many of the angels of the Celestial Court during her lifetime.[2] Her writings tell us that the Guardian Angels of those who are called to intense suffering on earth wear a crown and are attired in red. The Guardian Angels of innocent souls wear white and are assigned as servants for such souls. The Guardian Angels of children are exquisitely lovely. They are dressed in blue and always are seen with their hands folded in prayer.[3]

As each soul progresses higher on the path to sanctity, angels from the higher Choirs are assigned to join that soul's Guardian Angel. In the higher realms of spiritual awareness people are guarded by a team of angels.[4] The path is more difficult as the ascent to God continues because the attacks of the rebel spirits are more vicious and cunning. Obviously the stakes are higher. The ministrations of the angelic team defend a soul's attempts to conform more perfectly to the will of God. This behavior enrages the rebel spirits, who loathe the will of God.[5]

The greatest obstacle between God and the human soul is a deformed self-will that is incapable of discerning truth. Self-will, centered in our own narrow view of reality, impedes our vision of God. Often such a problem is the result of generational bondage. Some babies imbibe counterfeit truth with their mother's milk. From generation to generation evil forces have sown the seeds of darkness with deceit, distortion, and destruction. The power of the holy angels mediates between human difficulties centered in such ignorance, or even malevolence, and the will of God.

Some Guardian Angels bear the sad misfortune of being assigned to a person who irrevocably and with full knowledge chooses to rebel against the will of God. Jesus became obedient unto death to teach His Followers the holy virtue of obedience to the will of God under all circumstances. Sometimes God's Will is difficult, even painful. He has promised that nothing He allows in our lives is too difficult for us. God's Angels of Consolation are standing by, waiting to help us and to comfort us. Those who use Angel Power in times of stress, sorrow, and pain are clothed in the mystery of God's Love and Providence. Those who rebel against God's Will forever forfeit the privilege of dwelling in Paradise with God, the Angels, the Prophets, the Blessed Mother, and the Saints.

Evil begets evil. When those who malevolently and permanently have chosen to disobey God, with full knowledge of the consequences, pass through the portal of death, they are met by evil spirits, who are waiting to claim them. They are shackled and brought as prey to the kingdom of death, despair, degradation, and depravity. Therein each person is assigned a personal demon by Satan to torture and punish him or her forever.[6] In such tragedy the Guardian

Angel, though deprived of the eternal companionship of his beloved earth person, is assigned as a special guard of the Queen of Angels, where he praises the Justice of God for all eternity. In this way the Guardian Angel is not deprived of joy.[7]

Angels are the ambassadors and ministers of God to the entire cosmos, including the earth and each one of us. There is a Guardian Angel for every person ever conceived or to be conceived. Other angels have never been, nor ever will be, a Guardian Angel to anyone of the earth. All the angels of the entire cosmos continuously surround the people of the earth.

The human heart sometimes hears the voice of God in the wind:

> *Dare to be alone with Me.*
> *Go beyond your senses.*
> *You can get only glimpses of Me with your senses.*

Precious "aloneness" is those still moments when we allow the longing in our being to cry out for the Divine. Our Guardian Angel is then joined by countless angels of the vast, unfathomable Celestial Court. As the angels of God draw exceedingly near to us, our eyes and our ears open to the wonder of God's Presence in all that lives. Everyone comes to that moment of precious aloneness. When it happens, the chains of illusion drop from human consciousness. The enchantment is over, and Truth brings real freedom.

Angels in the Park

Bonnie was overwrought. "Please, God, don't let Daddy die!" was all she could think or say. Nobody at the hospital even noticed the slight, almost frail-looking young teenager as she walked back and forth, back and forth, between the intensive care unit and the lounge. There was no kind hand to comfort her. There was no soothing voice to speak of God's Love in what looked like human tragedy.

"Please, God, don't let Daddy die now!" she bargained. "Just give him another year." Bonnie thought of all the things she and her dad had planned to do, all the words she'd planned to speak to him, and her heart broke.

Abruptly the loudspeaker announced that visiting hours were over. Bonnie looked out the window at the darkness, and suddenly she realized the lateness of the hour. "The streetcar!" Bonnie panicked. She had no money to take the streetcar. Hunger was such an intimate part of her life now that she was almost used to its pain. The cold, dark streets of Pittsburgh in 1930 were another matter. Home was five miles away.

There was no choice now for Bonnie. She had to leave the hospital. She pulled her spring coat close to her shivering body. The rain turned to slush, and little particles of ice began to cling to Bonnie's hair. There were no streetlamps, and Bonnie walked in the dark, using her memory of the roads. "I'll take the shortcut through the park," she decided, as the lights of the city diminished.

Suddenly Bonnie saw the eyes of a leering man. Unknown to Bonnie, he was one of the inhabitants of the park. There were actually quite a few who camped there. Homeless, penniless outcasts, they begged on the streets by day, then drank, cursed, and robbed by night. Bonnie froze. She was aware that she was in mortal danger. "Blessed Mother of Jesus, help me!" a tiny voice from long ago whispered in Bonnie's memory.

At first Bonnie didn't see the huge dogs. But the man with the leering eyes did. He began to curse. It was then that Bonnie smelled the whiskey. There were several men now, and they all began to curse as two Doberman pinschers, one on either side of Bonnie, bared their teeth. Dirty, drunken men seemed to be everywhere.

The dogs! They were almost as tall as Bonnie! They were ferocious, and the leering men knew it. To Bonnie they were like angels from on high. Slowly she dared to put one foot in front of the other. The dogs moved with her. Then she walked another step. The dogs accompanied her. Confidence entered the young girl's heart. Her courage rested in the big dogs. "Let's go!" she said quietly.

Bonnie and the two dogs walked through the park. They climbed the hill to Bonnie's house. Bonnie recited: "Hail Mary, full of grace, the Lord is with you. Blessed are you among women and blessed is the fruit of your womb, Jesus. Holy Mary, Mother of God, pray for us sinners, now and at the hour of our death. Amen." Over and over again the words of the Hail Mary, first spoken by Saint Gabriel the Archangel, tumbled from her lips. The dogs seemed to understand.

The porch light was dim through the sleet. But what a welcome sight! In spite of all the expenses of her father's illness, she, her mother, and younger brothers still had a home. Bonnie reached over to pet the sleek heads of the two Dobermans.

"God is good!" she sighed as she climbed the steps of the small porch. Her mother opened the door. "Bonnie! Thank God you are finally home! I sent my Guardian Angel to get you!"

Bonnie instinctively reached to pet the Dobermans. There were no dogs beside her. She was totally alone. Or was she?

The Great Archangel Gabriel

Saint Gabriel the Archangel is traditionally characterized in art and literature as an Angel of Pure Light whose beauty is a clear mirror of God's Beauty. He carries the lily as his symbol.[8] This Archangel has the privilege of facilitating a great love for God's Will in souls who seek and receive his assistance. Once we realize our role in God's Plan and access Angel Power, our soul blossoms like a spring bud in the warmth of God's Love and Providence.

The great and humble Archangel Gabriel has traditionally been identified as the Guardian Angel of the sacred humanity of Jesus. It is wondrous to contemplate the human beauty and charisma of Jesus Christ and the admiration of the angels He commanded. Jesus always saw God's Beauty in each person He approached or who approached Him. No one was scorned by Him. No one was condemned by Him. He brought love and beauty and healing to every person and circumstance He encountered. He acknowledged the dignity of all our Father's children. He brought abundance. The unfathomable beauty of Jesus is so attractive to truth seekers that two thousand years after His Crucifixion and Resurrection we only begin to understand the power of the authentic Christian call. It is inextricably linked to Angel Power.

Saint Gabriel the Archangel, as the Guardian Angel of the human nature of Christ, cared for Jesus during His Agony in the garden.[9] Along with countless millions of angels the Archangel Gabriel stood by while Roman soldiers allowed themselves to be Satan's victims. These demonized warriors savagely attacked the face, head, and body of Jesus, believing they were destroying forever His Love, Power, and Beauty. Little did they realize Whom they crucified. Jesus knew, and He loved them unconditionally. The angels knew, too, and they saw everything.

Each of us, from time to time, in lesser or greater degree, has the same problem the Roman soldiers so dramatically manifested. We do not see Truth. We really do not know one another. We often do not see the beauty, dignity, and nobility of ourselves, or of God's Other children, who share with us His Earth, His Cosmos, His Heavens, His Will. For that reason the majestic virtue of obedience to the great Cosmic Law of the Creator stands as a mighty sentinel of Truth.

The Archangel Gabriel remained with Jesus as He hung on the cross and died. All who were present were amazed at the dignity, virtue, and love that the God-man exhibited. His full humanity was clothed in His Full Divinity.

Christ's own Angel Power enveloped the suffering, dying Jesus, and with Him the whole world from the beginning to the end.

On the great morning of the resurrection of Jesus from the dead, the power and eternal beauty of the Resurrected Christ routed the defeated rebel spirits. Jesus Christ triumphs. The entire cosmos shines with His Victory. The great Archangel Gabriel is known as the Angel of the Resurrection and the Ascension.[10] Each Guardian Angel of every person who has ever lived is affiliated with Gabriel in the promise of eternal life through Jesus.

Humankind, from the beginning, has desired to see God, Who is the beginning of no beginning and the end of no end. Jesus, the great living human icon of the unseen God, came to earth clothed in the flesh of the Blessed Virgin Mary: the most Holy One came forth from her womb a tiny, helpless babe, fully human and fully God (John 1:14). Those who gaze at His Face see Mary's features, and possibly those of all her ancestors in various ways. But they see more than human features: those who look at Jesus see pure love, for God is love.

In the human life of Jesus Christ, Angel Power reached its zenith. The billions of angels who attended Jesus mirror eternally God's Unconditional Love that shines in the mystery of Christ's life, death, and resurrection. God Himself came down to earth to care for humankind. Do the angels dare do less? Do His children dare do less for one another?

One Special Angel

Each Guardian Angel is unique and different from any other Guardian Angel, just as you and I are unique and different from any other person. Each Guardian Angel has distinctly defined characteristics, just as you and I enjoy distinctly defined characteristics. Those who really know their Guardian Angel intimately have a great blessing.

Since our Guardian Angel is such a precious part of our interior life, the more in touch with our own depths we are, the more familiar we are with the voice and movements of our Guardian Angel. Usually it requires deep self-knowledge to discern the unique characteristics and pulsations of our Guardian Angel. Of course such knowledge can come from direct infusions of Divine Grace. Our understanding of the ways of angels flows from Divine Grace offered to us during the daily circumstances and surprises that confront us in the process of an entire lifetime.

Since our Guardian Angel is selected for us by God Himself, the relationship between each of us and our own Guardian Angel is intended to be the most loving and intimate of all possible relationships. Our Guardian Angel knows absolutely everything about us. The love of each Guardian Angel is total and unchanging, no matter what we do or say, because it is rooted in God's Love. Our Guardian Angel loves us unconditionally and forever.

Some people spend their entire life on earth with only vague notions of their Guardian Angel, who in truth is their dearest friend and inseparable life companion. How happy is that glorious moment when a human awakens to the vast, limitless horizons of the spirit world. There each becomes acquainted with his or her inseparable life companion, who is a blessed spirit of pure love. This beautiful creature has been with us from the beginning. How much there is to share when the veil is lifted!

It is the mission and job of our Guardian Angel to accompany us during the entire span of our life on earth. Guardian Angels act as divinely appointed personal spiritual guides and teachers. People who recognize their Guardian Angel's presence acquire true joy in accessing Angel Power in the world.

Saint Thomas Aquinas is called the great Angelic Doctor. He said, "Because our present life [on earth] is a sort of road home along which many dangers, internal and external, lie in wait, an angel guard is appointed for each person as long as he [or she] is a wayfarer. But when he [or she] reaches the end of the road he [or she] will no longer have a guardian angel, but either an angel who shares with him [or her] the Kingdom, or a demon punishing him [or her] in hell."[11]

The more conscious we become of the spirit world, the more intimate our relationship with our Guardian Angel becomes. As we access the presence of our Guardian Angel more and more, a reciprocal relationship of exquisite love flowers. It stands to reason that we labor to become like those we love and admire. As we develop in the ability to access Angel Power, we begin to take on the characteristics of our Guardian Angel.

Remember Ben from chapter 2? Ben has a highly developed relationship

with his Guardian Angel, Michael, who is his best friend and counselor. It is the height of wisdom to befriend the angels, because they are God's proven and trusted Friends. The Bible story of Joshua depicts God's Angels interceding before the Throne of God and pointing out the good deeds of His People. Joshua's Guardian Angel actually defended him from Divine Justice, and he was spared chastisement (Zechariah 3:15). God sometimes may allow His Justice to be assuaged by our Guardian Angels, who defend and protect us against misfortune.

Those who consciously befriend and help their Guardian Angel while the sun shines have nothing to fear. Like begets like. Those who adopt the characteristics of their Guardian Angel fit comfortably within the Nine Choirs of Angels of Paradise. Perhaps if we are very still, our Guardian Angel will tell us more. Solitude is the place where our Guardian Angel speaks loudest.

God is so serious in His Commitment to drench the earth in His Divine Mercy that He has not only assigned a personal Guardian Angel to each soul on earth but in addition He has assigned a special Guardian Angel to every nation, city, village, and hamlet. These Guardian Angels of places are of great importance. As people begin to request and receive the protection and joy that the Guardian Angels of places can produce, much of the pain and sorrow of the world that is the rotten fruit of the demons will be eliminated. Indifference begets indifference.

Our Guardian Angel, who always stands beside us while we are on the earth, simultaneously and continuously sees the face of God and wants us to see

On facing page: Guardian Angels appear to us when we need them.

God too. All the angels eternally love, praise, and glorify God.[12] This is the behavior they long to see in us because they realize it is the source and means of our happiness. Nothing we ask of our Guardian Angel is inappropriate if the request will bring us closer to God's Will for us.

Meditation

I AM IN THE WORLD.

My Voice,
Though echoing now in the
Silence of
People's hearts,
Shall be heard.
Not one of the
Little ones
Entrusted to Me by
My Father,
Shall be lost.

Guardian Angel Prayer

(TO ACCESS THE CELESTIAL COURT)

Draw near to me, O Holy Angel of God, my own Blessed
    Spirit of Beauty and Power and Truth,
To keep a constant watch and ever listen,
To my needs and dreams and longings.

Obtain a pure heart for me,
Your Chosen One.
As you wait upon me in silence and calm,
Bring all the angels of the Celestial Court to me
That I too may know God as truth and light and beauty.

All you Angels of the Heavenly Nine Choirs,
Teach me of your love at every moment.
Sing to me the mysteries of your wisdom.
Breathe on me the strength of your holy commitment.

Change my meager human heart into fire
That rises up to heaven like a flame that never ends

Until it consumes the path that blinds me to Your Loving
      Presence.

O Holy Angels of God, my own Blessed Spirits of Beauty and
Tranquillity,
Lift me quickly and tenderly to the Mountain of Truth,
Where my Home beckons now in the Glorious Land of
      Eternal Love.
Amen

Chapter Seven

Angels in Danger,
Distress, and Sorrow

✠

Then going out he went, as was his custom, to the Mount of Olives, and the disciples followed him. When he arrived at the place he said to them, "Pray that you may not undergo the test." After withdrawing about a stone's throw from them and kneeling, he prayed, saying, "Father, if you are willing, take this cup away from me; still, not my will but yours be done." And to strengthen him an angel from heaven appeared to him.

—LUKE 22:39–43

God is a tender and merciful Father Who loves His children unconditionally. That love empowers His Angels to be where and what His children need at all times. Angels are God's Instruments of protection, consolation, and enlightenment. They strengthen our understanding. They impart to us the awareness of Truth.

Because angels are pure spirits, they do not have material bodies the way human beings do. We are both body and spirit. The structure of an angel is perfectly transparent.[1] For a human to see an angel, it is necessary for the angel to assume a corporeal shape. Any angel is quite capable of doing so when such action is part of God's Will.[2] We never really know when an angel or two are among us in physical form unless we possess exquisite Angel Power. Even then we can never be sure as long as we dwell in our human body.

The angels are not permitted to act directly upon our decision making. They can, however, influence us indirectly by presenting images to our imagination. By their own natural power angels are able to assume some visible form that allows us to see what is not really there, as the two dogs who accompanied Bonnie through the park taught her.[3] Their behavior is always motivated by love and obedience to God's will.

It is to the pure of heart that the Lord, through His Angels, offers clear-sightedness.[4] Purity of heart, a heart that beats for God alone, is the desire to do God's Will, regardless of the personal cost. Those with clear vision recognize that all creation, all people on earth and in Heaven, live before the face of God at all times. For those who love Him all things work together for good.

God is Love and Power and Beauty. He wills that His children live in abundance, peace, joy, and reciprocal love. God's Love is so great, however, that He respects the human freedom He has given to each of His children. It is through the holy angels that God's Power and Love and Beauty are mediated to His children.[5] Those who seek Him find Him and His Paths of Reciprocal Love. Those who ignore or abandon His Ways reap the benefits of the kingdom of illusion. Angel Power brings the Kingdom of God on earth, for the kiss of angels awakens us to Truth.

Long before God made the world, He fashioned a marvelous eternal Plan for His People of the earth that includes the angels. During the thousands of years of recorded history all people have participated in that Plan with varying degrees of awareness. As people awaken to the reality of God's Plan in their lives, the mystery of the presence of angels in the world gradually unfolds. Such awareness unmasks the power and deceit of the evil spirits. As their traps are uncovered, the bondage of evil is broken.

People of all races, nations, beliefs, and ages claim to have personal spiritual experiences that bring to human understanding awareness of the world that lies beyond the five senses. Many people, especially in times of difficulty or distress, are actually able to see angels or observe their handiwork. People have also had visions of the Prophets, the Lord Jesus Christ, the Blessed Virgin Mary, and the Saints.

Many venerated apparitions span thousands of years and are recorded in all the holy books. They are distinctly prophetic, always pointing the faithful to profound hope in the mystery of God's Eternal, Unconditional Love and Abiding Providential Presence throughout Creation. The longings and the dreams and prayers of hope they inspire encompass the wisdom of the ages. Each generation has claimed access to the Divine.

Angel Power on Ski Patrol

Jeff loved the mountains near Lake Tahoe. Lake Tahoe was as close to Paradise as he ever wanted to get. College was nearly over. Jeff had no real desire to join what he believed was the "ant-like workforce." From his vantage point men worked, struggled, and died. He wanted to ski, do recreational drugs, bike-ride in the mountains, enjoy beautiful women, and look for love. The problem he faced that day on the mountain was how to make his dreams come true.

He saw the majesty of the snow-covered mountain peaks. He breathed in deep breaths of clean mountain air. The chill in the air made the bristles of his mustache tingle. The silence was noisy that March morning on the top of Snow Mass. Suddenly Jeff felt lonely. There in the splendor of Creation he panicked. The glory of the moment, he realized, was a fleeting memory already.

Jeff pounded his poles into the crunchy snow and catapulted his body into the wind in a downward power push. Faster and faster he skied. "God, take me now!" he dared the biting cold that slapped his bare cheeks. Abruptly the path narrowed, and before Jeff could alter his downward thrust, the tip of his ski hit the pole of a marker flag. The impact thrust Jeff into the air at a ninety-degree angle. He shot over the side of the mountain in a straight drop of one hundred feet.

Exhilaration gave way to shock, shock became terror. Then, suddenly, Jeff felt overwhelmed with peace in the face of certain death. He saw beautiful colors and experienced a warm joy covering him like a blanket of love. In the radiant light that surrounded him Jeff heard the following words:

*"My beloved son, I have never left you. I am always with
you. I shall never leave you unless you send Me away."*

Jeff heard his spirit cry, "I have looked for you everywhere! Nothing
makes sense. Nothing has value." A deep voice of intense compassion from
long ago spoke gently in the recesses of Jeff's memory:

"All I have is yours,
My beloved son,
if
you choose Me,
My life, My ways."

The last thing Jeff heard before he hit the snow was his own shriek: "Father, save me!"

Slowly the light came into Jeff's awareness. He was at the bottom of a
gorge. The snow was silently falling. Great big flakes quickly covered him. He
couldn't move. He had no pain. He was not cold. He heard a voice that
sounded like clear bells far away:

"I am Gabriel the Archangel.
Your Father in Heaven loves you.
He has heard your call.
Your life has great value.

Follow me to the path of life.
I shall lead you to Jesus.
His Words, His Life, are the path of Truth."

When Jeff awakened, he was in a ski-patrol helicopter. The doctors who cared for him arranged for drug rehabilitation as well as physical therapy to restore some mobility to Jeff's crippled legs. He is now a physical therapist in San Francisco who paints and writes poetry about angels in his free time. He is married to a nursery school teacher and does volunteer work at the local drug and alcohol rehabilitation center. He and his wife do-si-do at their weekly square dance. Their daughter, Mary, loves to square-dance too. Their infant son, Gabriel, is still too young to dance.

Angel Power at the Seaport

Charintorn, whose name means "heavenly water," was one of many children in a family that practiced few if any of the tenets of the Buddhist faith of her ancestors. They lived in the remote mountains of Thailand near the border of Burma, where the roses grow profusely and are as large as the green grapefruits of the port cities.

When she was quite young, Charintorn was sold by her father into a house of prostitution. Her "salary" was sent to her impoverished family each month (or so the straw boss claimed). It was a dreary, degrading life for Charintorn. She thought about her family often and found some relief in believing that her misfortune in some macabre way was helping them.

One night as Charintorn fell into a heartbroken sleep, she dreamed of a kind man with eternal eyes of love and compassion. He told her His Name was Jesus and that He loved her. He told her He would stay with her always and that He would protect her. He told her she was more beautiful and more precious than the blooming roses she loved so much. Charintorn fell into a deep and refreshing sleep that eased her weariness. The next day her straw boss sent her with a few of his older "employees" to a busy port city to meet a ship that was scheduled to land that evening.

As Charintorn walked along the sidewalk near the port, she saw a poster of Jesus in the window of an evangelical mission. "My Master!" she gasped. "There is my Master!" she cried, becoming quite hysterical. Suddenly two burly missionaries stepped out into the noonday sun. They saw the sobbing girl as she knelt before the picture in their storefront crying, "Jesus! Jesus save me!"

"What's going on here?" they demanded as a rough man and an even more cruel woman tried to pry the sobbing girl from the mission.

"She belongs to us! Move away," the woman commanded.

"Not so fast, ma'am," the missionary with the soft Texas drawl cautioned. "Sounds to me like she might just belong to the Lord Jesus."

The missionaries bought Charintorn that day.

She and her husband, a retired physicist, now live in Boston, where Charintorn works as an English-language teacher for foreign students.

Angel Power and the Ten Commandments

Dreams and apparitions of the Lord, the Blessed Virgin Mary, the angels, the Prophets, and the Saints have traditionally called humanity to certain rules of enlightenment. The underlying themes of the apparitions express fundamental principles of the cosmos, ordained by God to be comprehended and observed.

One such apparition is the basis upon which many Judeo-Christian nations are founded. The Decalogue is based upon Moses' experience on Mount Sinai with what was, in the widest sense, a type of "apparition" or "visible presence" of the Unseen God. The mountain "blazed to the very sky with fire and was enveloped in a dense black cloud" (Deuteronomy 4:11). From the midst of the fire the Lord God spoke to Moses, commanding him to observe and to teach others to observe His Mighty Ten Commandments of Love. These Commandments are great walls of safety behind which God's Faithful children live in peace.

Angels help God's People remain faithful to His Ten Commandments of Love, the great Decalogue:

> *1. I, the LORD, am your God, who brought you out of the land of Egypt, that place of slavery. You shall not have other gods besides me. You shall not carve idols for yourselves in the shape of anything in the sky above or on the earth below or in the waters beneath the earth; you shall not bow down before them or worship them. For I,*

the LORD, your God, am a jealous God, inflicting
punishment for their father's wickedness on the children of
those who hate me, down to the third and fourth
generation; but bestowing mercy down to the thousandth
generation, on the children of those who love me and keep
my commandments.

2. You shall not take the name of the LORD, your
God, in vain. For the LORD will not leave unpunished him
who takes His name in vain.

3. Take care to keep holy the sabbath day as the
LORD, your God, commanded you. . . .

4. Honor your father and mother, as the LORD, your
God, has commanded you, that you may have a long life
and prosperity in the land which the LORD, your God, is
giving you.

5. You shall not kill.

6. You shall not commit adultery.

7. You shall not steal.

8. You shall not bear dishonest witness against your
neighbor.

9. You shall not covet your neighbor's wife.

10. You shall not desire your neighbor's house or
field . . . nor anything that belongs to him.

—Deuteronomy 5:6–21

A man asked Jesus Christ to explain the great Commandments of His Father:

> One of the scribes, when he came forward and heard them disputing and saw how well he had answered them, asked him, "Which is the first of all the commandments?" Jesus replied, "The first is this: 'Hear O Israel! The Lord our God is Lord alone! You shall love the Lord your God with all your heart, with all your soul, with all your mind, and with all your strength.' The second is this: 'You shall love your neighbor as yourself.' There is no other commandment greater than these."
>
> —Mark 12:28–31

Those who would access Angel Power understand this great Cosmic Law of the Creator of all that is seen and unseen. It is the power of God, of the Holy Spirit of Love, that makes the burden of obedience light. It is the power of the Holy Spirit of Love that frees humankind from the bondage of the kingdom of illusion.

Countless heroes throughout human history, at great personal cost, bring the commandment of love to places of darkness. Charintorn was rescued by human "angels" of God's Mercy. Angel Power carries us on the wings of God's Merciful Love. Mercy begets mercy. Those who love are "angels" of God's Mercy.

Angel Power in Sickness

Saint Raphael the Archangel is known as the Angel of God's Mercy and Consolation in earthly trials. He is the angel of health and has great power and desire to help the sick and the broken in their sufferings.

The pastor of a church in Cleveland was praying one evening for a parishioner's son who lay in critical condition in a nearby hospital. With each passing hour life drained from the boy, yet no one was able to diagnose his illness. In his distress the pastor got into his car and drove to the hospital.

Entering the intensive care unit, the pastor immediately fell to his knees and prayed, "God our Father, in the name of the Lord Jesus Christ, please send whatever angelic help this young man and those who care for him need to solve all his medical problems. I particularly entrust him to the care of Your Great Archangel, Saint Raphael, the patron of healing. Amen." Within forty-eight hours the hospital was able, through an affiliate in Europe, to identify the mysterious virus that afflicted the young boy. Many scientists all over the world were involved in the diagnosis. Each scientist and each nation was accompanied by a Guardian Angel. Mighty levels of Angel Power brought quick and effective treatment for the young man. He was restored to perfect health. Was it the pastor's prayer that accessed Angel Power?

※✕※

Saint Raphael is the Angel Protector of families and of happy, fruitful, and lasting marriages. He is also the Angel Protector of successful business ventures

(Tobit 9:1–5). Saint Raphael has enormous power to assist souls who enter into religious rituals for the glory of God. His power is immense during the reception of the Sacraments, especially, Sacramental Confession.[6] The primary characteristic of Saint Raphael the Archangel is kindness.

This gracious Archangel is powerful in obtaining help for those with loved ones who refuse or are unable to love God. It is humility and selflessness that open hearts to the great love of God. For those who do not experience those virtues, prayer to Saint Raphael on their behalf has been quite effective throughout history.

Angel Power in Betrayal

A betrayed wife began to ask the great Archangel Raphael to intercede on behalf of her estranged husband. Each day she prayed that no harm would come to the father of her five children. Their neighbors in Houston spoke of the laughing young women who were seen in the company of her husband, who had risen to prominence in his job. Eventually the company transferred her husband to a distant city.

As feelings of rejection and negativity closed in on her, the betrayed wife prayed more frequently and intensely. She still loved her husband and hoped he would come to his senses, but his phone calls soon ceased, and she had no way of opening his heart. She recognized the pain that her children were silently enduring. She knew the commandments. Not one unkind word was ever heard from the sorrowful woman. Her children's self-esteem depended on their recognition that they had worth, that they were not abandoned. Their father's choices were not their choices. Fortunately her husband's company had enlightened policies that were financially benevolent to families, and divorce had never been discussed.

The betrayed wife may or may not have been aware that God's Sacraments are the balm that heals the poison of sin. The Sacrament of matrimony, when it is fully embraced by both parties in a marriage, heals the sin of lust. It purifies the appetites of lust and greed and avarice and sloth. It heals self-love.

The mother taught her children that they are like Jesus when they honor their parents. She read to them from the Bible how Jesus underwent His passion and crucifixion to honor His Father. Jesus endured all, in front of His Blessed Mother, to honor God by demonstrating great love for God's children, by respecting their choices, even though they tortured and killed Him. She insisted that her children honor their father in word and prayer.

The children, as they, too, read the Bible, began to recognize that the authenticity of their own love and faithfulness was at stake in the way they chose to respond to their family crisis. They focused on Jesus. By His Obedience to the Fourth Commandment, which He understood perfectly, Jesus honored His Father by honoring the choices of God's children. The children of the betrayed wife realized that their own father had made some choices that hurt and injured them. To be like Jesus, they were called to high levels of forgiveness in their relationship with their own father.

The mother refused to allow herself the empty "luxury" of judging her husband's motives. She recognized that she could not hold her husband to a higher standard than God does. She knew, from the Bible, that God expects His children to love and forgive all wrongs. Only prayer gave her the strength she needed to face each day in peace. The mother prayed fervently every morning and evening with her children for their father. Slowly she realized that it was not God's Will for anyone passively to accept whatever degradation another's choices might occasion. The more she prayed, the stronger she became. A quiet wellspring of hope began to flow copiously from her heart to the hearts of her children.

One cold morning as the sun began to break through the frost-covered windows, a great light flooded the little bedroom where the mother and her children knelt in prayer. In the immense light an outline of the glorious angel was evident, and certain family members clearly heard the following words:

> *I am the Archangel Raphael.*
> *Family prayer pleases the Heart of God.*
> *As I stand before the Throne of God,*
> *I present your humble obedience and trust in*
> *His mercy, His kindness, His promises.*
> *You each shall know the goodness of God.*
> *Even in the final moments of human life,*
> *God's mercy covers the path of His children.*

Know that all prayers are acceptable to God.

All prayer is heard.

God always rewards trust.

Have no fear.

Trust always the mercy of God.

Before noon the betrayed wife received a certified letter from her estranged husband's employer. It read in part, "Though your husband's accidental death was quite sudden, I know that you will all be consoled by the knowledge that he died thanking God for each of you and asked that his memory be filled with thoughts of the mercy of God. The pension and life insurance programs of his employment are generous. . . ."

Prayer and obedience to God's Commandments combine to form an arrow that pierces the Heart of God. John's first Letter reminds the contemporary of Jesus' teachings about the Heart of God our Father:

"Beloved, if [our] hearts do not condemn us, we have confidence in God and receive from him whatever we ask, because we keep his commandments and do what pleases him" (1 John 3:21–22).

In some circumstances great prayer, coupled with meticulous obedience to the Commandments, remains unanswered. In such circumstances the person who struggles so heroically shall rejoice for all eternity as the value of such faith-filled suffering unfolds.

Saint Raphael the Archangel

The following is said to be a message from the great Archangel Raphael about why some prayers are apparently not answered by God:

> There are cares and trials which God never removes, because He wishes that people continue their prayers. It is most pleasing to God when people constantly but with complete resignation beg Him for relief in their sufferings. Since God is infinitely good and merciful towards men, He leaves nothing unrewarded, and He gives to such people graces so precious that men could not imagine them, although apparently He leaves their prayers unanswered. It will be one of our great joys in Heaven when we learn with what care and love God surrounded us while on earth. The value of trials is immeasurable. Trials are the greatest of all earthly gifts and graces of God—and men seldom realize this and so little appreciate their great value.[7]

It is part of God's Plan for us that we seek comfort from His Angels while we are pilgrims on the earth. God wants us to form an intimate relationship with the angels. He sends them to us to guide us and guard us, especially in times of sorrow and difficulty. Those with seemingly insurmountable problems, such as the betrayed wife was forced to confront, need all the Angel

Power they can gather to cope with their sorrows. Often the choices of others impact us and force us to endure tribulations that require heroic levels of Angel Power. People caught in a war zone or in the path of a hurricane have no control over their circumstances. Human relationships, too, can suddenly erupt into a torrent of distress. Prayer is the means by which untold thousands of invisible blessed spirits of power and love surround us to protect and strengthen us. Prayer activates Angel Power.

When we ignore angels, our silence around them and to them is not pleasing to God. It is His Will that we become aware of His Heavenly Kingdom on earth. God's Glories are hidden everywhere. Obedience to His Commandments, plus prayer and trust in God's Mercy, give us eyes to see those glories. It is in the simple things that we experience true beauty.

Every day, all over the world, little acts of kindness among people blossom like a whiff of spring in the darkness of winter. The laughter of babies brings a promise of better tomorrows. Girls and boys find joy in the dreams of eternal love that sing in their longings. Sudden scientific breakthroughs augur hope for the conquest of disease and physical misfortune. Self-sacrificing people in every occupation and calling who struggle for virtue and moral integrity express the deepest promise of the nobility of the human person.

Angel Power in the Post Office

Scripture tells us that God has made His Angels "winds, and flaming fire"(Hebrews 1:17). Angels have a Divine Appointment to watch over, guard, and guide us. Sometimes the presence of angels is witnessed as great clouds of smoke or experienced as the lovely fragrance of flowers or burning incense. Angels speak to us in dreams, too. These phenomena are the loving Creator's little gifts to boost faith. All people do experience the effects of Angel Power, even though many are not yet consciously aware of the presence of the angels.

The universal understanding regarding Angels is that their inspirations lead us to virtue. However, we need to cooperate with virtuous inspirations. Each positive good act lifts us to a purer awareness of Truth. Normal people seek happiness. Some achieve it, others do not. Every action has consequences that either benefit or deter from the personal quest for happiness. True happiness is rooted in faithfulness to Truth, no matter the cost. It is the splendor of Truth alone that brings peace, joy, and love to human beings. The splendor of Truth is light.[8]

David is a famous international finance lawyer. His mother had a powerful and hidden prayer life that David rarely speaks about. Once, a precious document was lost that involved many lives and many millions of dollars. David was frantic. He was responsible for the safekeeping of the original document.

On facing page: Untold thousands of invisible blessed spirits of power and love surround us to protect and strengthen us.

Everyone in the New York firm where he worked and colleagues on two continents were quietly helping David reconstruct events in hopes that the document would surface. Without the document David's reputation and career were finished.

Finally desperate, David found the synagogue of his youth. He entered when he believed no one would see him. He prayed as his father had taught him. He prayed fervently for the retrieval of the lost document. Then he left.

Several nights later David had a wonderful dream. He saw his mother. She was not old as she had been at her death. She was young and quite beautiful. How happy she was! Seeing her so blissful caused David to experience the elation that little children know so well when real happiness is attainable.

"Mother, how happy I am to see you!" he exclaimed in the dream. She was hugging him and swinging him in the air and kissing his face and curly hair just as he remembered her doing when he was a tiny boy. He was laughing and she was laughing with him. How loved David knew he was!

"My little son," she suddenly interrupted, "call the central post office. They are holding your document."

David awoke with a start. He had no knowledge of why the central post office had his document, but he was certain it was there. It was difficult to wait until morning.

Finally the doors of the post office opened, and David was there. David's vital document was in a batch of misaddressed mail scheduled to be destroyed the following week.

Angel Power Transforms Adversity

David had accessed Angel Power. Was it his mother David saw in the dream or was it an angel? God permits angels to take on corporeal shape when it is part of His Will for the well-being of His children. Angels are a gift of God's love. Angels do not frighten God's children. They come to us in ways we are able to comprehend. They reward proper behavior.

David's problem became a blessing. It brought him the opportunity to worship, adore, and petition the Great God of Abraham. A reward was the renewal of his memories of childhood love. A joy was the shared concern and efforts of his friends who joined in his sorrow and searched for his lost document. All worked together in service of justice. All were trying to live God's Will. God is never outdone in generosity.

The Great Commandments are recognized, in varying degrees of awareness, as the Cosmic Rule of the Great God of Abraham Whom Jesus introduced as Our Father (Mark 12:29–31). Jesus explained,

> *If you live according to My Teaching,*
> *you are truly My Disciples;*
> *then you will know the Truth,*
> *and the Truth will set you free.*
> *—John 8:31–32*

God's Commandments, the great cosmic rules, are contained in all the sacred books. They are written on the hearts of all people. Those who obey God reap His Bounty, as David and his friends realized. They experienced the generosity of Angel Power. Throughout the centuries, as night follows day, enlightened mankind has realized that disobedience to the Commandments, referred to as sin (bad choices), blurs truth. It is deep, unrepentant sin that dulls the voice of God in our awareness. A humble and contrite heart God will not scorn. A repentant heart is God's Great Treasure. A reward for true repentance is Angel Power.

Virtuous people who offer their lives to protect the integrity of the great Cosmic Law of the Creator inspire the multitudes to strive for virtue, for equality, and for a just liberty among all the peoples of the earth. When a person finds peace, joy, and love, he or she lives in harmony with God, the angels, and earth and all its inhabitants. Can there be any other worthy goal? It is attainable through Angel Power.

Meditation

I Am Your Father.
I am Love.
I fill your world with My Angels.

Call to Me.
Sing to Me.
Praise Me.

I hear all prayer.
All prayer has value.
I answer all prayer.

My Arms are outstretched.
I await your arrival.
Come to Me.

Prayer

God our Father, You are Lord of Hosts
and Savior of humankind.
Almighty, Merciful, Eternal, Unchanging, Redemptive Love,
Come swiftly upon the wings of the wind
and dwell in us now
and forever.
Amen

All you angels of the Lord of Hosts,
Guard mightily these Temples of the Lord,
our human bodies, created from the dust,
in the love of the Eternal Love.

In us He chooses to dwell, for we are His.
He Who is mighty has done great things for us.
Holy, holy, holy is His Name.
Amen

Part II

The Forces of
Evil and
the Kingdom
of Illusion

Then war broke out in heaven; Michael and his angels battled against the dragon.

The dragon and its angels fought back, but they did not prevail and there was no longer any place for them in heaven. The huge dragon, the ancient serpent, who is called the Devil and Satan, who deceived the whole world, was thrown down to earth, and its angels were thrown down with it.

—REVELATION 12:7–9

Chapter Eight

The Evil Spirits

✠

But woe to you, earth and sea, for the Devil has come down to you in great fury, for he knows he has but a short time.

—REVELATION 12:12

The Bible takes for granted that humankind has a powerful enemy known as the Dragon, Satan, the Adversary, the Accuser, the Great Deceiver, the Devil. All disciplines admit we are at present ignorant about the mystery of iniquity. Mythological battles between good and evil teach the great lessons by which wise choices in life are learned that protect against the snares of evil. Modern stories, as well, prepare us to recognize evil. J.R.R. Tolkien's depiction of evil, personified in the character Gollum in *The Hobbit* and *The Lord of the Rings* trilogy, gives deep insight into situations devoid of God's protection. In *The Screwtape Letters* C. S. Lewis offers profound observations of the behavior of evil spirits as they take advantage of human ignorance, weakness, naïveté, and laziness.

The quintessential battle of good versus evil has raged from the beginning of time in the face of the ultimate truth: God is Peace, Joy, and Love. All flows from His Hand. Truth alone sets angels and humankind free. Angels help us in the quest for true freedom. Obedience to the will of God is the key that gives us access to that state of eternal bliss. Obedience to the will of God is the test of all angels and humans. Those who pass the test enjoy the Empyrean Valleys of Paradise forever.

Holy angels are celestial beings who always obey God's Will. They live in harmony with all creation and are one with God in all that is. But those spirits who refuse to obey God's Will dwell in an eternal, unchanging state of rage against God and those who obey Him. Many refer to these rebellious spiritual beings as devils, evil spirits, or evil forces. The disobedient spirits, filled with hatred and rage, by their own choice no longer have access to the goodness and mercy of God. They have no understanding whatsoever of peace. Joy is incomprehensible to them. They are living hate. Love therefore is anathema to them.

Evil spirits wage continuous war against people who dwell on the earth. They despise the earth, too, and consciously seek to spoil it. Evil spirits especially attack anyone who consciously seeks to obey the will of God. They use people who allow themselves to be available to them to torture others. Sometimes their malevolence is easily apparent; sometimes it is not. Misfortune occurs in many ways that are fraught with deception and counterfeit joy, peace, and love.

The forces of evil connive incessantly to inflict injury upon those who love God's Ways or bear God's Gifts in large quantity. They have a personal vendetta against anyone whose talents are a sign of the goodness of God. From brilliant scientists to accomplished athletes, no one is immune. Evil spirits constantly harass. They tempt and try to lure people out from behind the walled safety of the great Cosmic Law with the enticement of counterfeit truth.

People throughout history have been brought down by counterfeit truth disguised as normal, even preferred behavior. No class or group is exempt. Many great statesmen, artists, writers, scientists, business leaders, musicians, athletes, and countless others throughout the centuries have fallen into the pit of devastation that underlies counterfeit truth. How many people have embraced smoking with no understanding of the cruel damage it brings to their lungs? How many have become addicted to drugs, fed by the false promise of harmless pleasure or relaxation? How many have suffered, gone mad, or died horrible deaths because of the misfortune acquired in deceitful relationships? It is not beyond the capacity of evil spirits to stir up brutal wars to prevent great light from saturating the world, as the world wars of this century demonstrate.

Other calling cards of the evil spirits include the side effects and aftermath of war: destruction, poverty, illness, insanity, premature death, suicide, broken families, crippled relationships. Demons derive pleasure in mocking truth, love, peace, joy, purity, beauty, and all virtue. They incessantly tempt with the allure of counterfeit truth. The more faithful or gifted a person is, the more the forces of evil attack.

It requires discernment and wisdom to recognize counterfeit truth. Those who rely upon the strength of holy angels are better able to avoid the death grip of illusion. Those who access Angel Power are lifted out of the morass of counterfeit truth by the angels.

Though bad choices sometimes feel marvelous for the moment, they are toxic and bring certain death to the dreams and aspirations that dwell in all hearts. Bad choices destroy if they are not recognized and corrected.

Angels have the power of God to remedy all the problems that human weakness occasions. Because they are exquisitely humble, angels do not interfere in the gift of freedom God has bestowed upon His children. From generation to generation unrecognized mistakes and bad choices chain much of humanity in self-made bondage. For those who love God, even all the mistakes and bad choices eventually work together for good. Unfortunately the price is often patiently endured suffering.

To access Angel Power is to walk the path of enlightenment. Angel Power is a means to learn from mistakes and assiduously avoid repeating them. Those who access Angel Power recognize that the process requires immense discipline and prayer. The tools to access the power of the angels are great gifts of God's Mercy (see chapter 14).

God never rewards iniquity, and evil spirits know it. They disguise iniquity by dressing it in counterfeit truth. Evil spirits lead God's children deep into the valley of worldly comforts, worldly prizes, worldly pleasures. Then they gloat as God's children become sick on the poison of illusion and die.

Demons connive to addict God's children to comfort. Their temptations are designed to destroy human freedom. Pleasure becomes counterfeit truth when God's children are led to imbibe and ingest substances that are seriously injurious to health, to seek fame such that they do not rest as they pursue it, to strive for success such that they lose family unity to maintain it, to hoard wealth such that their funds benefit no one, to usurp power such that they destroy people.

Evil spirits corrupt God's Harmony, God's Peace. The French Court at Versailles has taught subsequent generations much. Worldly pleasure as a destiny is illusion. Ungoverned human appetites are insatiable. Human comfort and pleasure never satisfy. No one in the history of the world has ever had enough power, money, sex, food, wine, or possessions. What pleases a person today loses its allure tomorrow. Those who are addicted to worldly comfort and pleasure grow sick at heart and die.

God is restoring His Kingdom on earth. God sees all hearts. God alone fills His children's hearts. Those with sick hearts who learn to pray for pure hearts are healed. God blesses the work of hands that labor for His Ways, His Plan. Those who labor to please God eat honey and drink sweet water. No sour wine is their portion. Those who labor to please their appetites go hungry. Their lips are parched. They never get their fill. Those who live to please God alone have Heaven on earth, and the demons know it. That is their reason for hawking counterfeit truth with such vengeance.

Those who know angels well come to the fullness of love. They live in the generosity of God's Kingdom and are one with the angels in harmony and serenity. Those who love live consciously in God's Presence and experience His Abiding Love. They have eyes to see God and ears to hear God. Such awareness of God's Presence is pure contemplation achieved through prayer and fasting. A teenager who experiences pure contemplation, remarked as she enjoyed an evening with friends in a disco, "God is pretty hard to forget."[1]

Prayer and fasting unmask the cannibalism of mere worldly pleasure as an end in itself. Images of the Emperor Nero, who played his violin as Rome burned, or Queen Marie Antoinette, who suggested that the starving French people eat cake when they couldn't even afford to eat bread, demonstrate the sickness that infects those who are totally preoccupied with their own personal agenda of gratification. Unjust worldly pleasure taints the purity of God's image in our soul. Undisciplined worldly pleasure dims our eyes to His Presence in the world. Unbalanced worldly pleasure creates a din in our ears that silences God's Voice. Voluntary prayer and fasting open us to the joys of God's Presence in the world and the dignity and beauty of one another. Prayer and fasting are reciprocal communication with God, angels, and one another. Worldly comfort and pleasure are unilateral perceptions. They occur within the boundary of our own body and imagination. Pleasure not shared and reciprocated is not pleasure. It is illusion. It causes those who stare at an abyss actually to believe the abyss stares back.

People do strive for comfort. We experience God smiling upon us when we appreciate His Gifts, including the soft wool of the sheep, the sweet taste of the orange, the warm water that fills our baths, the company of loving friends. A person becomes too comfortable, however, when luxury takes his senses away from God and focuses them on himself. A person who lives only for himself destroys himself.

God's Ways are living, flowing splendor, light, beauty, and power. God's Ways are clear to those who choose to avoid people, places, and things that blur God's Kingdom. Proper choices and the help of angels allow us to find God's Ways.

There is protection from the snares of evil only as long as God's children remain within the walled safety of God's Commandments, the great Cosmic Law. Spiritual discipline and discernment are indispensable for those who would overcome the constant bombardment of the forces of evil. No human can withstand such attacks alone.

The Bible story of Job is one of the great literary masterpieces of the Old Testament that deals with the mystery and reality of why misfortune and suffering attack good people. The words of Job shed light upon the immense power of faithful choices by God's children.

One day, when the sons of God came to present themselves before the Lord, Satan also came among them. And the Lord said to Satan, "Whence do you come?" Then Satan answered the Lord and said, "From roaming the earth and patrolling it." And the Lord said to Satan, "Have you noticed my servant Job, and that there is no one on earth like him, blameless and upright, fearing God and avoiding evil?"

But Satan answered the Lord and said, "Is it for nothing that Job is God-fearing? Have you not surrounded him and his family and all that he has with your protection? You have blessed the work of his hands, and his livestock are spread over the land. But now put forth your hand and touch anything that he has, and surely he will blaspheme you to your face." And the Lord said to Satan, "Behold, all that he has is in your power" (Job 1:6–12).

Though Job was severely tested by Satan, he persevered in God's Ways, saying,

"Naked I came forth from my mother's womb,
and naked shall I go back again.
The Lord gave and the Lord has taken away;
blessed be the name of the Lord!" (Job 1:21)
The Lord rewarded his faithfulness by restoring Job's prosperity,
  giving him twice as much as he had (Job 42:7–17).

When Christ was on earth, the sorrowful and broken-hearted flocked to Him seeking freedom from demonic oppression (Mark 9:17–29). The horrific human condition encountered by Jesus has not vanished. The battle of good versus evil continues to rage as it has raged throughout the ages. Truth alone yields freedom. The pursuit of Truth is the ultimate goal of human life.

Counterfeit truth, the kingdom of illusion, casts a spell over those who gaze upon its allures. Students who refuse to study and prefer leisure embrace counterfeit truth. Employees who do their jobs haphazardly embrace counterfeit truth. Employers who mistreat their employees or misrepresent their operations embrace counterfeit truth. Governments that disregard the well-being of the people embrace counterfeit truth. The dignity, beauty, peace, and abundance of those who embrace counterfeit truth is eroded, sometimes subtly and oftentimes brutally.[2]

The splendor of Truth is light.[3] Counterfeit truth is darkness. Truth must be synonymous with goodness, just as counterfeit truth must be synonymous with evil. As M. Scott Peck writes: "The truly good are they who in times of stress do not desert their integrity, their maturity, their sensitivity. Nobility might be defined as the capacity not to regress in response to degradation, not to become blunted in the face of pain, to tolerate the agonizing and remain intact."[4]

Angels are pure spirits of Truth. Their power and love guide humans to pure Truth. People who would draw near pure Truth must become "truly good." There is ample evidence throughout recorded history that God has given angels mediated power to govern the whole cosmos.[5] Now we are embodied spirits who dwell within the cosmos on the planet Earth. Angels constantly tend to the spiritual well-being of all who seek Truth while we dwell on earth. When our bodies die, we are human spirits with an eternal destiny. Those who are glorified dwell with angels in Paradise forever. Those who are not glorified remain slaves of evil spirits.

A Journey to Hell

Throughout the ages there have been allegorical depictions of Heaven, Purgatory, and Hell presented in the sacred texts and in art, literature, and music. Blessed M. Faustina Kowalska, though she was minimally educated, was a spiritually privileged woman who died in Poland in 1939. She wrote in her *Diary* of many visits with Jesus, the Blessed Virgin Mary, and the angels in visible form during her short life. The Vatican has investigated thoroughly and pays much attention to the life and messages of Blessed Faustina, who has quickly been raised to the last rung of the ascent toward canonization.

Faustina visited Heaven, Hell, and Purgatory with the angels. Her description of Hell is similar to those of other famous visionaries throughout the centuries and is reminiscent of Dante's *Inferno*, a book that has inspired hundreds of generations of artists and musicians. Blessed Faustina discovered different levels in Hell. There are also various levels in Purgatory and in Heaven, as the Nine Choirs of Angels demonstrate.[6] The following is an excerpt from Faustina's description of Hell:

> Today, I was led by an Angel to the chasms of hell. It is a place of great torture; how awesomely large and extensive it is! The kinds of torture I saw: the first torture that constitutes hell is the loss of God; the second is perpetual remorse of conscience; the third is that one's condition will never change; the fourth is the fire that

will penetrate the soul without destroying it—a terrible suffering, since it is a purely spiritual fire, lit by God's anger.

[Author's note: God's anger is not like the anger of human beings. God has no cruelty. God's anger cleanses. God condemns no one to Hell. People choose Hell. Those who choose Hell for themselves desire nothing but eternal hatred and revenge. Those who choose Hell for themselves, because of its eternal properties, are never again able to experience the beauty, order, and tranquillity of the Empyrean Valleys of Paradise, where God and His Faithful Ones dwell.]

The fifth torture is continual darkness and a terrible suffocating smell, and, despite the darkness, the devils and the souls of the damned see each other and all the evil, both of others and of their own; the sixth torture is the constant company of Satan; the seventh torture is horrible despair, hatred of God, vile words, curses and blasphemies. These are the tortures suffered by all the damned together, but that is not the end of the sufferings. There are special tortures destined for particular souls. These are the torments of the senses. Each soul undergoes terrible and indescribable sufferings, related to the manner in which it has sinned. There are caverns and pits of torture where one form of agony differs from another. . . . [The unrepentant sinner] will be tortured throughout all eternity, in

those senses he made use of to sin. I am writing this at the command of God, so that no soul may find an excuse by saying
there is no hell, or that nobody has ever been there, and so no
one can say what it is like.[7]

Evil in Places and Things

The demons work relentlessly to turn the planet Earth into a living hell for
those who succumb to their empty promises and lies. It takes faith in God's
Promises and the humility to pray together as children of God to access Angel
Power. Angel Power routes the forces of evil. Love energy begets love energy.

A word of caution: Only God is worthy of worship. A holy angel recognizes that truth. No creature or created object deserves worship. There is much
evidence that evil spirits desire to be worshiped. Throughout the centuries be-
lievers have been quite sensitive to such demonic traits, recognizing that demons
actually sometimes hide in statues and shrines to receive the worship of the
faithful. Demons are able to latch on to inanimate objects. Certain places on
earth are considered cursed. There is charged negative energy. Evil spirits are so
hungry for adulation that they pretend to be the object of authentic worship.
Illusion is very much embroidered in the personality of demons.

The Guardian Angels of places defend and guard us on many levels
when we actively obtain their protection. Places and objects used in religious
rituals are frequently blessed to assure the continuing protection of holy angels.

The human need for Angel Power is absolute and flows from God's Divine Plan for us.

Just as people recognize beauty, order, and peace in places, most people have had the experience of encountering a place or a situation that is actually mired in distortion and negative energy. In such circumstances it is wise to access Angel Power immediately by beginning to communicate with your Guardian Angel. There are countless millions of holy angels at the beck and call of our Guardian Angels waiting to love and serve us by keeping us within the gentle, faithful protection of God. He promised that in times of trouble or distress, those who ask shall receive the help of the angels of the Celestial Court. The gift of wisdom invites all the Angels of the Nine Choirs to fly to our immediate and continued assistance.

The demons are hyperactive, always drawing attention to themselves, to sorrow, to misfortune, to half-truths, to outright deceptions. Evil spirits have angelic powers that have been darkened. They are quite capable of wreaking havoc in the world in which we live. Their counterfeit truth is presented to us in countless deceptive ways. Often such distortion is accepted by those who do not have the gift of discernment. Angel Power allows us to differentiate between things of God and things devoid of the goodness of God. The sad plight of those who accept counterfeit truth is entwined in the useless suffering that envelops their lives and the lives of those they are able to influence. Angel Power guards us from the lies of the evil spirits. God gives His children freedom. Satan places his followers in bondage.

Good thoughts and inspirations come from holy angels. Angels, however, are forbidden to infringe on our freedom. Rebel spirits have no such restriction upon them. Angels wait to be invited to participate in our lives. Rebel spirits are rude, greedy, and officious. Their goal is to harm people: to destroy health, relationships, families, livelihoods, businesses, villages, cities, and nations. They never sleep. They are always on the prowl. It takes awareness every moment to hear the inspirations of holy angels.

Demonic Cults

Often when holy angels intervene to help those who do not pray, it is because of the prayers of others. A family in Oregon suffered the misfortune of losing their teenage son to a demonic cult. He moved out of his family home, indulged in satanic orgies, became severely addicted to drugs, and craved heavy-metal rock music. He joined the entourage of a satanic rock group. The youth in this group exchanged their bodies for drugs and alcohol.

The parents and twin brother of the teenager were devastated. They were powerless to rescue their son and brother from such a pain-driven life. Several families joined together to form a prayer group on behalf of the teenager. Many months passed. There was no word of the boy.

As winter came on, the youngster began to be excluded from the rock-group entourage. Finally he demanded to know why he was being omitted from the orgies. A person with supernatural powers committed to the evil forces was in charge of deciding who entered the parties and who was excluded. Barring his entrance, the person told him, "If you must know, there is a huge angel of the Lord with you. I will not allow this angel assigned to you to come into our territory."

The prayer and fasting of his parents, twin brother, and the prayer group had accessed Angel Power on behalf of the misguided young teenager. Soon he returned to his family and received the help he needed to overcome his addictions. Why do some get Angel Power and others do not? Why do some people love enough to pray and fast and sacrifice for others? There is much mystery; there is also much pain and much joy. Awareness heals.

Meditation

I long for you.
Bring your heart to Me.
I am your Father.
Every circumstance of your life occurs before My Face.
Hear Me in the wind.
Sense My Presence hovering about you always.

Notice the flowering of love among you, My children.
Your suffering waters the sweet buds of love in many lives.
Allow others the privilege of service.
In your brokenness they are nurtured in love and trust of My Ways.

You are being weaned from dependence upon yourselves to
*   dependence upon Me.*
You have been led to the path.
Now you must follow Me.
Come back to the Kingdom of love and service.

Eliminate all the trappings of wealth and luxury in your lives now.
Stay in My Presence, dear children.
All is well.

Prayer

Angels of God
All you mighty spirits of wisdom and truth,
Energize my mind that I may
Comprehend God's loving Plan for me.

Angels of God
All you gracious spirits of peace and joy,
Enlighten my thinking that I may
Accept the gifts of God for me each day.

Angels of God
All you powerful protectors of God's holy will,
Guide my decisions that I may
Enter into conscious awareness of your loving presence
now and forever. Amen

Chapter Nine

The Twentieth Century

This is the convenant which I will make . . . says the LORD. *I will place my law within them, and write it upon their hearts; I will be their God, and they shall be my people. . . . All, from the least to the greatest, shall know me, says the* LORD, *for I will forgive their evildoing and remember their sin no more.*

—JEREMIAH 31:33–34

Secrets

God's love for us is so great that He allows Angels, Prophets, Saints, visions, dreams, signs, circumstances, and events to warn His People when they rebel from His protective ordinances. The sacred texts are filled with such messages from Heaven. Those who have heeded His Voice have historically enjoyed His Protection. God's great fatherly love for His People is unconditional. Those who do not heed His Voice fall into error. They bring much suffering upon themselves and their children because they do not recognize Truth.

The secrets of the Divine Plan are written in nature, in biology, and even in the hearts of all human beings. Illusion masks the obvious. The poison of illusion enchants its captives. Those who are enchanted frequently do not recognize evil. Love breaks the power of evil. Peace flows from the River of Love. The River of Love flows from the Heart of God.

God tests those who claim to love Him, for love untested is no love at all. God manifests Himself to those souls who are disposed to receive Him. A jealous God, He will have no other person, place, or thing before Him. Those who would remain faithful to His Edicts do find the pearl of great price. The search is a process that often is excruciating. Those who seek God find Him. To find Him is to taste the sweetness of eternal Paradise. Nothing else satisfies.

The Angels' Test

Just as we undergo testing each minute of every day, constantly choosing between right and wrong behavior and attitude, so also, long ago before the world was made, angels were tested. Because angels have a heightened capacity to recognize Truth, they were tested only once. God gave angels exquisite minds, capable of discerning Truth. Angels were given the opportunity to choose Truth. God also gives minds to us so that we may know what good means. It is written upon our hearts. We are able to form judgments rooted in Truth.

Because God is Pure Love, He forces Himself upon neither angel nor man. God invites. God woos. Angels were invited to choose His Ways. So also are we invited to choose His Ways. Those who will not choose God and His Ways are left with the consequences of their decision.

The amazing story of the rebellion of the angels is recorded in the Bible. Similar human rebellions are repeated daily out of ignorance, weakness, indifference, or even malevolence. All God's Gifts are for our use in His Kingdom. Should we take God's Gifts for ourselves alone, they become anchors lodged in hell. When we use God's Gifts for the glory of His Kingdom, they become stepping-stones to Paradise. All belongs to God but our freedom, which ends at death when we choose our destiny based on how we have lived.

The story about the rebellion of Satan and his followers has been recounted for centuries. Each generation experiences new twists of the same deceptions.

One day in the Kingdom of God, before the world was made, it is said that Lucifer was permitted to see a woman named Mary. She was created by God out of the dust of the earth. Then Lucifer saw that God clothed Himself in her flesh and dwelled on the planet Earth.

God is unchanging. Though He dwelt in a human body as a full human being on the earth, He remained always God. Lucifer's imagination was inflamed. Fully Divine and fully human! Why not fully Divine and fully angel? Why Mary? Why not Lucifer? After all, he reasoned, wasn't he the best and the brightest of all angels?

Lucifer brooded. He became filled with jealousy and envy toward human beings. He greatly desired a union of God and creature to be his own prize. Lucifer seethed. He reasoned that as God's finest creature he was therefore entitled. He was absolutely certain, with his finite mind and limited vision, that he was the most beautiful of all God's Creation. He venerated his self-perception and wanted all others to venerate it too. He refused to look at himself against the infinite horizon of God's Will.

It is said that Lucifer, equipped with such self-love rooted in illusion, confidently approached the holy Throne of God to negotiate on his own behalf. He was informed that his desire was not God's Will. God had another plan that involves angels and all humankind.

Lucifer continued to brood. He slowly glimpsed the unfathomable love God has for human beings. Lucifer learned more of God's Will. All generations would call the Virgin Mary blessed, for God would become her Divine Son so that all people might be children of God.

Lucifer believed he was far more gifted than the lowly Virgin Mary. God, however, sees all His Creatures as they are, as they were, and as they can become as a result of their choices.

Lucifer could not comprehend why God would endow a mere female human being with His divine presence as a human person. He rationalized

God's Plan as logical only if such a union would occur with him, through him, or in him. His position hardened as he gleaned fragments of God's Plan.

First God would fashion a chosen people among His Family of human beings created out of the dust of the earth. He would speak to them through Prophets and other enlightened men and women. He would give them unique rules and special ways to show their love for Him. He would send angels to guard His People and to do battle for them. Lucifer and other angels would be expected to serve God's People who remain obedient to His Laws.

Lucifer was beginning to understand the Plan, and he didn't like it at all. The woman Mary would bear God's own Son and name Him Jesus. Through Jesus, God raises faithful humans higher than the angels, even though they are made of earth-dust. God has breathed His Own Life into each human being. He wills that those who remain faithful to His Plan are His Own children and Heirs to His Kingdom. No angel enjoys such an immense gift of God's Love.

The truth is that angels, with all their power and gifts, are intended from all eternity to serve God by serving humans in their quest for divine childhood. Lucifer may or may not have known that Jesus, the God-man, came to earth out of love to show humans how to live and how to die faithful to God's Plan. Those who follow the pattern of Jesus' life choose to climb the spiritual mountain of love. At its summit they cross over to the waiting arms of their Eternal Father and dwell with Him forever. The cross of Christ is the triumphant sign of that covenant and crossing over.

Lucifer, it is said, was shocked to realize that God fully intended to become one with the people of the earth in Jesus Christ so that they would be His Own Biological children, flesh of His Flesh and bone of His Bone.

What dignity for all humanity! Jesus' life, death, and resurrection makes it possible for God's children to have Heaven even on the earth and forever after with Him as His children in Paradise. Saint Paul explained that through Jesus we are able to experience an intimate life with God, more elevated than any of the angels.

Lucifer, at some point in time, recognized Jesus as the suffering servant of humanity. He became consumed with envy, which ripened into immutable hatred. Focusing on his own gifts, making his own intellect and knowledge the arbiter of Truth, Lucifer reared up in boiling pride and hurled his fiat in the face of the Holy, ever tranquil Trinity: "I will not serve you in a form (Jesus Christ, fully human and fully Divine) that far beneath me." Lucifer did not mind the Divine Nature. That he understood. It was the human nature that infuriated him.

Many other highly gifted angels were drawn into Lucifer's pride, envy, jealousy, and hatred. They rebelled mightily at worshiping God in human form. They discarded the virtues of humility and obedience to the will of God. With those virtues they would have been capable of serving human beings as children of God and heirs to His Kingdom of Love.

The splendor of Truth is that God's Will is done on earth and everywhere else. His creatures, both angels and humans, choose their level of participation in God's Will. Lucifer and his followers so preferred their own power and authority that they chose to withdraw from the celestial realms of peace, joy, love, patience, kindness, goodness, faith, mildness, and temperance. They knew the decision was irrevocable. Then they gorged themselves on abomination and hatred. Their insignia are pride, envy, jealousy, anger, gluttony, lust, and sloth.

Faithful, obedient angels, led by the Archangel Saint Michael and clothed in wisdom, understanding, knowledge, counsel, fortitude, piety, and fear of the Lord, escorted the mutineers from heaven. The humility of holy angels was so intense that the devils raced from their presence, hurling themselves into the fire of eternal revenge. Such is self-made hell.[1]

The chief of the rebel spirits despised God's Will for him. His very name, Lucifer, given to him by God, means "light-bearer." It is an announcement of the Plan of God for His children of the earth. God wills that angels bear the light of God to humankind by means of interior illumination.

To announce his eternal break with God's Will, Lucifer chose a new name for himself, Satan, which means prince of eternal darkness. The name *Satan* announces the rebellious spirit's self-aggrandized independence from God's Plan. *Satan* is the sign of the disobedient one's authority, as an angel of darkness and despair, over those children of God who knowingly and willingly choose to disobey God's Plan for them.[2]

When God's precious children, at the ongoing suggestion of Satan, unknowingly look at one another through his eyes, they see people of differing size, race, culture, economic or educational background, class, religion or nationality, and they unwittingly perceive, "I do not love you. I will not serve you, because you are far beneath me." That attitude leads to war in the heart, war in the home, war in the cities, nations, and world.

God's children do love His Power, Might, and Largess. Many, however, do not comprehend His Humility. Some do not accept His Word and will not follow His Ways. Jesus taught all the world by His Own life, Death, and Resurrection. The sacred books contain God's Way.

The power of the forces of evil in modern times is evidenced by the chaos and conflict in the world among all peoples. Many today, as in the past, do not accept God's Will. Many do not like His Plan.

The angelic rebellion against God in Heaven led by Lucifer was a battle of the wills: God's Will versus the will of His Angels. The most endowed angel, with gifts of intellect and beauty, Lucifer preened in his perception of his own importance. He lost sight of the Gift-giver in the heat of his self-love. The proud Lucifer forcefully announced, "It is I and no other who shall be like the Most High!"[3]

By that decision, made with full knowledge of all the consequences, Lucifer chose to forfeit his relationship with God forever. He preferred to lead in his own self-made kingdom, where, taking his gifts for himself, he is chief. Lucifer the light-bearer extinguished his light by his calculated choice.

In the face of Satan's rebellion, Michael the Archangel chose to "kneel" in the presence of God. He immediately submitted his mind to the yoke of obedience to God's Will when confronted with the sacred humanity of God in Jesus Christ. Acknowledging the eternal sovereignty of his Creator, he cried out those immortal words of obedience and loyalty: "Who is like God?"

God rewarded the faithful Archangel Michael and endowed him with immense power and beauty. He stands before the Throne of the Eternal Father and is the great ambassador of the Almighty Creator of all that is seen and unseen.

Other angels joined Michael the Archangel. Their humble submission to God so infuriated Satan, consumed with his inflamed desires to lead and rule, that he preferred to reign in hell rather than serve anyone or anything. *"Then war broke out in heaven; Michael and his angels battled against the dragon. The dragon and its angels fought back, but they did not prevail and there was no longer any place for them in heaven"* (Revelation 12:7–8). The triumphant weapons of the Archangel Michael and his followers are obedience, humility, love, and service.

As for Satan? *Obedience? Humility? Gratitude? Service?* To the rebel spirit, the words are anathema. Gathering his followers, perhaps as many as one-third of all the angels, the evil one stomped out of Heaven cursing his Source. It was holiness that cast Satan out of Heaven and down to the earth, where he does battle with the children of God.

Imagine Satan's fury at God's Plan for His Earth children who remain faithful! His revenge and rage are contained in all the evil in the world. The intensity of the pain and sorrow of life on earth signals the fierceness of the struggle by invisible forces to discredit and destroy God's Beautiful People. Human suffering is a sign of the immense need for everyone to access the power of holy angels as the battle for souls rages on every continent.

Though Jesus' life, death, and resurrection marked the climax of the battle, the war is not yet over. Saint Paul enlightened the Hebrews with the following words:

"But to which of the angels has [God] ever said: 'Sit at my right hand until I make your enemies your footstool?' Are they [angels] not all ministering spirits sent to serve, for the sake of those who are to inherit salvation?"—Hebrews 1:13–14

The value of each person on this earth is inestimable. There is hope for everyone. No one is excluded. Jesus said,

"See that you do not despise one of these little ones, for I say to you that their angels in heaven always look upon the face of my heavenly Father."—Matthew 18:10

All people of the earth are created by God the Father. Before He made the world, He knew each of us who would ever live. He called to each of us when our turn to live in the world arrived. We came forth out of the Love in His Heart, overflowing with love. All are invited to Divine Childhood as children of the Father. Each day, at every moment, we choose whom we obey, whom we follow. We choose whom we emulate. Angel Power crushes the barriers of pride, rebellion, and hatred. We become what we observe. We are what we choose.

Will the battle between good and evil that has raged on the earth from the beginning finish in these times? There are many indications that the times portend extraordinary graces and tremendous change in the world as we now know it.

Some modern scholars and scientists are studying the approximately fourteen thousand "readings" or prophecies of the late Edgar Cayce. He predicted changes in the seacoast lines, a magnetic shift reversing the Poles, and the breakup of the land mass of the western United States by seismic eruptions before the end of the century. Enough of his earlier predictions have proved to be accurate that interest in his vision remains keen in certain circles. Followers of the sixteenth-century prophet Nostradamus claim that he predicted a world-ending holocaust in 1999. Today the possibility exists, as never before in recorded history, for mankind to destroy the planet. More than thirty countries now have plutonium available. Terrorists have few scruples. Hope is not an attribute of the doomsayers.

As the twentieth century comes to an end, thinking people are awakening to the presence of holy angels. They are finding new relationships with one another that are blessed with the vision of a noble purpose for life and for the planet. Humanity stands on the brink of the Era of Holy Angels. A glorious time of peace, joy, and love is breaking through the ancient and eroding crust of selfish illusion. The winds of peace are stirring mightily in the hearts of those who love.

God is pure love. His Will and His Ways triumph. Mercy is the antidote to the poison of illusion. Angel Power is the rainbow of God's mercy. The pot of gold is purified love that spills over the earth, the cosmos, and the heavens.

Meditation

War is a punishment for sins.
War among people would cease if My children would Pray and
Fast.

The war today is with the unseen world.
The battle for souls is fierce.
The Weapons of Victory are Prayer and Fasting.

My Love for each of you, My children,
Is beyond your capacity to comprehend now.

My World is a rich Playground for My children.
Soon there will be no evil hearts left on My Playground.

Prayer

Saint Gabriel the Archangel,
Mighty Spirit of Kindness, Beauty, and Love,
Enter deeply into my life with all your blessed gifts.
Surround me always with God's Holy Peace.

Saint Gabriel the Archangel,
Mighty Spirit of Kindness, Beauty, and Love,
Hold dear all those whom I love.
Make us invisible to our enemies.
Gather us near as you fill us with God's Holy Joy.

Saint Gabriel the Archangel,
Mighty Spirit of Kindness, Beauty, and Love,
Carry us on the wings of the wind to the Mountain of Eternal
     Tranquillity.

Abide with us there until that wondrous day
When at last we meet in the Kingdom of Love. Amen

Part III

The Nine Choirs of Angels

After this I had a vision of an open door to heaven, and I heard the trumpetlike voice that had spoken to me before, saying, "Come up here and I will show you what must happen afterwards." At once I was caught up in spirit. A throne was there in heaven, and on the throne sat one whose appearance sparkled like jasper and carnelian. Around the throne was a halo as brilliant as an emerald. Surrounding the throne I saw twenty-four other thrones on which twenty-four elders sat, dressed in white garments and with gold crowns on their heads. From the throne came flashes of lightning, rumblings, and peals of thunder. Seven flaming torches burned in front of the throne, which are the seven spirits of God. In front of the throne was something that resembled a sea of glass like crystal.

—REVELATION 4:1–6

Chapter Ten

Angels of Pure Goodness: Seraphim, Cherubim, and Thrones

⬛✖⬛

I saw the Lord seated on a high and lofty throne, with the train of his garment filling the temple. Seraphim were stationed above; each of them had six wings; with two they veiled their faces, with two they veiled their feet, and with two they hovered aloft.

"Holy, holy, holy is the Lord of hosts!" they cried one to the other. "All the earth is filled with his glory!" At the sound of that cry, the frame of the door shook and the house was filled with smoke.

—ISAIAH 6:1–4

The highest Choirs of Angels who dwell closest to the Throne of God are the Seraphim, the Cherubim, and the Thrones. All these holy angels are pure spirits of contemplation. Their holiness is so intense that the human mind is incapable of comprehending their levels of adoration and participation in the Divinity.

The Seraphim, Cherubim, and Thrones see pure goodness in its highest form. As they behold us, they view us in the light of God's Love. They always see us as the very best we can aspire to be. They long to help us to become pure goodness, for they know we shall then be truly happy.[1]

A most wonderful and dramatic angelic gift was given to humanity on the first Christmas. The Seraphim, Cherubim, and Thrones came and dwelled on the earth with the Lord Jesus Christ. They are His Messengers "not only among men but also among the lower angels who are more immediately charged with the government of earthly things."[2] Just as angels communicated the message of the birth of the King of Heaven to the shepherds on Christmas night, so, too, the highest-ranking angels communicate the mysteries of the Divine to the lesser angels, who then bring their tidings to the people of the earth.

Angels, as pure spirits, do not progress through the ranks of the Nine Choirs toward degrees of perfection. Higher angels have "a more perfect nature and keener intelligence," hence they have greater gifts of grace than the lesser angels.[3] They are mightier stewards of God than the less-endowed angels.

Saint Gregory the Great believed that each human is destined to join one of the ranks of the Nine Choirs of Angels, not as an angel but as God's children by cooperation with His Grace and perseverance.[4] Some scholars believe that each person is assigned a Guardian Angel from the Angelic Choir to which that individual is called. Such a Guardian Angel, in a spiritual way, prepares and teaches the soul for its place in one of the Nine Choirs of Paradise.

Saint Gregory described his perception of those human beings who could eventually share the ranks of the Seraphim as follows:

> Some [people] are set on fire by supernatural contemplation, and are filled with eager desire for their Creator alone. They no longer long for anything in this world, they are nourished by love for eternity alone, they thrust aside all earthly things; their hearts transcend every temporal thing; they love, they are on fire, they find rest in this fire; loving sets them on fire, and they enkindle others by their speech: those they touch with their words they instantly set on fire with love for God. What then should I call these people whose hearts, which have been turned into fire, are shining and burning, but Seraphim? They enlighten the heart's eyes with regard to things on high, and purify them of the rust of vices by tearful compunction. Where do these who burn so brightly with love for their Creator receive their calling's portion except among the number of the Seraphim.[5]

Seraphim

The Seraphim are Love Angels of the purest love. They are sometimes referred to as "burning fires of love." The intensity of their love is so great that it fills all creation in and through God. They reflect God's goodness, His Absolute Holiness. Each Seraphim reflects God in a special way, as do all angels. The Seraphim are angels of the purest and deepest created level of adoration. The intense love of the Seraphim protects the whole cosmos. It spills over and guards the entire world as it pours down through the lower Eight Choirs of Angels.

The first hierarchy of angels is so high, so august, so divinely intimate that no other creatures, save the Blessed Virgin Mary and Saint Michael the Archangel, have access to these angels directly. The Blessed Virgin Mary has direct access to God through Jesus without the intermediary of any angels. That is why she is known as the Queen of Angels. Saint Michael obtained his place through his great victory over the rebellious angels.

Saint Birgitta of Sweden was a most privileged soul who had conversations with angels. They explained to her that if we could see a Seraphim in all its glory, we would die of fright. Great artists have described them as bearing faces like lightning and clothes as blinding as snow. Their activity is ceaseless. Countless numbers of Seraphim surround the Throne of God glorifying His Splendor.

Some believe that those who are able to pray with fervent ardor to the level of a burning fire of love for God have their prayer transported by Seraphic angelic communications. Tradition teaches that the Blessed Virgin Mary, Queen of Humility, was and is capable of the greatest prayer intensity in the Kingdom of God. Her human will is a clear mirror of the will of God. She was taught and illuminated not only by angels but, more significantly, by her Divine Son Jesus. She lived fully conscious of God's Presence and, for thirty-three years, in God's Human Presence.

Those who invite the participation of the Blessed Mother in their prayer life experience tremendous interior illumination, for her life is overflowing with God's Presence. She, the Queen of Angels, sends the Seraphim to gather our prayers and transport them into her holy Immaculate Heart. Her pure, obedient love generates prayer intensity that draws her beyond the sphere of Divine Love guarded by the Seraphim. Her prayer requests are communicated directly to God through the power of her Son's love.

The Seraphim, as the highest of the Nine Choirs of Angels, surround the Blessed Mother, who, for most of humankind, remains God's Hidden Master-piece. All angels deeply revere and honor the Blessed Mother as their Queen, for she has the closest access to God of any creature. When she appears on the earth in public apparitions, the Seraphim of course accompany and surround her. Those who choose to participate in her public apparitions receive im-mense light because they are in the physical presence of the Blessed Mother and her entire Celestial Coterie of Seraphim.

Moses was an exquisitely advanced and highly enlightened person. He was so meticulously obedient to the voice of God that he bore within his person the expression of eternal youth. The Bible reminds us that although Moses was chronologically old, he had the body of a young man. Moses drew near the Living God. He stepped on Holy Ground. The glory of the Seraphim, Cherubim, and Thrones radiated from his face. Because he was so steeped in Divine Grace, he chose always to be highly conformed to God's Will. Moses reached the heights of meekness. Meekness is obedience to the will of God. The Seraphim, Cherubim, and Thrones draw near the meek.

The very name *Seraphim* means "ardor," for these angels are consumed with the fires of Divine Love.[6] Such depth of love comes from God alone. He alone chooses who drinks so deeply of His Divine Essence of Love. Where Seraphim dwell, humans dare not trespass, except by the mysterious invitation and power of the great Unknown.

Who reaches the summit of humility where the Seraphim, known as the Angels of Humility, silently adore the Holy of Holies? Through the mercy of God certain people of the earth dwell on the heights of the virtue of true humility.[7]

God alone is the source and sustainer of all that is. The gifts and life of the Seraphim are a mystery of God's Love, for they are the most sublime Choir of Angels. They are totally enflamed with the love of God and experience the greatest knowledge of God. For this reason they are the most humble of all angels.

Though all angels are totally happy, they can also enjoy "accidental" happiness. Each Guardian Angel, for all eternity, experiences the privilege of guarding only one soul during that individual's sojourn on the earth. When death comes and that soul is finally permitted to enter Heaven, the Guardian Angel's joy is beyond computation. The two are then companions in the realms of Paradise forever.[8]

Imagine the delight of those who are accompanied by a Seraphim. One such privileged soul was Blessed M. Faustina Kowalska. Before the outbreak of World War II she was traveling through Poland on a train once when, as she gazed out the window of the train, she became aware of angels who were poised above each church the train passed.

Because Sister Faustina had interior conversations with the Lord Jesus Christ, she asked Him why angels were hovering above the churches. Jesus informed her that each church has its own divinely appointed Angel Protector. She then asked the Lord why the angels were bowing. Jesus explained that Sister Faustina was accompanied by an invisible Seraphim. Each Guardian Angel of the churches of Poland bowed to the Seraphim who accompanied Sister Faustina because of her mission to spread devotion to the Divine Mercy of God in these times.[9]

From the experience of Blessed Faustina we may deduce that those who are entrusted by God with extraordinary, unique missions for the world may also be accompanied by angels of the Seraphic Choir.[10] The Seraphim receive the homage of the entire Celestial Court because of their burning love, which allows them the deepest angelic access to God.

The Seraphim are Love Angels of pure love. Their love is so great that it fills and protects the whole world. The Seraphim's pure love is like a beautiful coat of diamonds that covers the entire earth. On a starry night those who love begin to fathom the Seraphim's diamond coat glistening in the sky. No evil or harm can penetrate the Seraphim's glistening diamond coat. Seraphim protect the mystery of those who love with their own pure love.

Cherubim

The Celestial Court is beyond human comprehension. The angels are God's Treasure and our treasure too. The Hebrew word *Cherubim* was memorialized by the Prophet Ezekiel in a vision of Heaven that he described. He saw the Cherubim among the most exquisite, brilliant beings in all creation.

THE VISION: GOD ON THE CHERUBIM

The heavens opened, and I saw divine visions. . . . As I looked, a stormwind came from the North, a huge cloud with flashing fire [enveloped in brightness], from the midst of which [the midst of the fire] something gleamed like electrum. Within it were figures resembling four living creatures that looked like this: their form was human, but each had four faces and four wings. . . . They sparkled with a gleam like burnished bronze. . . . Over the heads of the living creatures, something like a firmament could be seen, seeming like glittering crystal, stretched straight out above their heads. Beneath the firmament their wings were stretched out, one toward the other. . . . Then I heard the sound of their wings, like the roaring of mighty waters, like the voice of the Almighty. When they moved, the sound of the tumult was like the din of an army. [And when they stood still, they lowered their wings.] Above the firmament over their heads something like a throne could be seen, looking like sapphire. Upon it was seated, up above, one who had the appearance of a man. Upward from what resembled his waist I saw what gleamed like electrum; downward from what resembled his waist I saw what looked like fire; he was surrounded with splendor. Like the bow which appears in the clouds on a rainy day was the splendor that surrounded him. Such was the vision of the glory of the LORD. —Ezekiel 1:1–26

Cherubims are the second highest Choir of Angels in all creation. The illumination they possess is beyond the human mind to comprehend. The higher the Choir of Angels, the greater is their wisdom and knowledge of Divine Truth. Such illumination operates like a beam of light. The Source is God. Those angels closest to God are able to absorb and possess the greatest intensity of Divine Light. They, in turn, beam their light to those lesser Choirs of Angels below them in capacity and receptivity.[11]

Only the unfathomable Seraphims contain more capacity to love, more wisdom and knowledge, power and might, humility and graciousness, than the glorious Cherubims. Is it any wonder that those who encounter an angel of the highest Choirs are temporarily blinded?

Cherubim are not the tiny, winged babies that artists are fond of painting. According to the Prophet Ezekiel, they are mighty spirits of knowledge, love, and intimacy with God. The Lord commanded His Chosen People to fashion two Cherubim figures of beaten gold to rest upon and serve as reminders of their power, presence, and protection of the Ark of the Covenant (Exodus 25:18–20). The Cherubim over the Ark formed the throne for the invisible Lord.

The Blessed Virgin Mary is the living Ark of the Covenant. It is she who bore the Son of God, Jesus Christ. It defies the imagination to comprehend the majesty of this hidden Holy Lady of God and the number of Seraphim and Cherubim who eternally accompany her. What love God has for His Human Family to fashion such a Blessed Mother for each of us.

Only the Hebrew Prophetess Anna and the Prophet Simeon had eyes to recognize her and her Divine Infant when she brought Him to the Temple in fulfillment to the law (Luke 2:22–38). Artists have consistently memorialized the Blessed Mother surrounded by Cherubim. Mysterious and wondrous are the ways of God.

The Bible describes the specifications for the sanctuary of King Solomon's Temple. They called for two figures of Cherubim, each ten cubits high, made of olive wood. Each wing measured five cubits, so that the space from wing tip to wing tip measured ten cubits. The Cherubim were identical in size and shape and were to be placed in the innermost part of the Temple with their wings spread wide to protect the entire enclosure. They were to be overlaid with gold (1 Kings 6:23–28).

When Solomon finally constructed his Temple, for the room of the Holy of Holies, he made two Cherubim figures of carved workmanship, which were then overlaid with gold. The wings of the Cherubim spanned twenty cubits. They stood upon their own feet, facing toward the nave. He made the veil of the Temple of violet, purple, crimson, and fine linen and had Cherubim embroidered upon it (2 Chronicles 3:14). Many churches in Christendom have huge Cherubim figures guarding the Tabernacle to remind the faithful of Truth.

From earliest times it was understood by revelation that the Cherubim are protectors of the inner chambers of the Divinity. Those who cultivate a relationship with angels have constant access to the Seraphim and Cherubim Choirs through their Guardian Angel.[12] Angel Power is a transport to the Heart of God.

God has made a covenant with His People. He desires to dwell within each of us. Jesus promised,

> *"Whoever loves Me will keep My Word, and My Father will love him [her], and We will come to him [her] and make our dwelling with him [her]" (John 14:23).*

Those who consciously allow God to dwell within them acknowledge the dignity of their human bodies as Sacred Temples of God. They recognize that they are surrounded with holy angels of the Seraphim and Cherubim Choirs and all the lesser Choirs, too, who pay homage to the presence of God within them. God made us for Himself. He is an All-consuming God, who allows no idols. God absolutely demands that we choose our destiny. Those who consciously permit the Creator of all that is seen and unseen to dwell within them access Angel Power over all the earth.

Thrones

The Thrones are the lowest-ranking angels within the highest group of the Nine Choirs. As Angels of Pure Goodness their primary characteristic is pure humility. It is their glorious humility that allows God to dispense His Magnificent Favors to creation through the Thrones. They are named Thrones because the very power of God that emanates to all that is created in the heavens and the cosmos and the earth "rests" upon the Thrones. All the lower Choirs of Angels are dependent upon the Thrones to access God.[13]

The Thrones are so filled with humility that God, who presides over them, carries out His Divine Justice through them.[14] God has so ordered His Creation that the wicked are punished by the very actions they perform. The Thrones, angels of God's justice, see Truth clearly. They mete out God's Will.

Every cosmic entity, from the smallest submicroscopic speck to the great-

est celestial body, depends for its very existence on the power of God. God is Truth. The humble Thrones are quite busy dispensing the justice and power of God to the Angelic Court in charge of the cosmos and the earth.

Many of humanity's finest moments have been steeped in the benevolence of the Thrones. History has been touched also by the justice of the Thrones. How sad a Guardian Angel must be to have the sorry duty of carrying out an assignment from the Justice of God given through the powerful Thrones. God has clearly given the angels authority to inflict punishment upon us. God is slow to anger and warns us always. Those who access Angel Power are usually able to discern God's Will. They spare their Guardian Angel much pain. Those who spare their Guardian Angel pain will be spared.

The angels comprehend the universe. They understand each of us. They love us with pure love. Because the Angels of Pure Goodness are endowed with the proven capacity to love in depths that are as yet incomprehensible, they are exquisite blessings in our lives and our world. They wait, day and night, to be invited into our lives, our decisions, our dreams and aspirations. The Angels of Pure Goodness have the might and the capacity to lift each of us to a glorious life of joy and intimacy with God that opens the portal to Heaven, even on earth.

On facing page: The glorious humility of the Thrones allows God to dispense His magnificent favors to Creation through them.

Meditation

Being selfless means loving God above all things He has created,
including yourself.
To love that way, you must know Him well.
Those who pray much know him.

Often it is only in extreme suffering, loneliness, and isolation that
human beings come to understand God.

God is Spirit. God is Truth.

Pray, My children. Fast, My children. Live in peace.
Pray for the gift of WISDOM.
Pray for the gift of DISCERNMENT.
Pray for the gift of SURRENDERING TO MY WILL.
Pray for the gift of FORTITUDE.
Pray for the gift of PATIENCE IN ADVERSITY.

Prayer*

Be praised, Merciful God,

One God in the Holy Trinity,

Unfathomable, Infinite, Incomprehensible,

Angels immersing themselves in You, their minds cannot
   comprehend You.

So they repeat without end their eternal: Holy.

Be glorified, O merciful Creator of ours, O Lord

Omnipotent, but full of compassion, inconceivable.

To love You is the mission of our existence,

Singing our eternal hymn:

Holy, Holy, Holy

Lord God of Power and Might,

Heaven and earth are full of Your Glory.

Hosanna. Hosanna. Hosanna in the Highest!

*Composed by the Blessed M. Faustina Kowalska of Poland.

Chapter Eleven

Angels of the Cosmos: Dominions, Powers, and Virtues

Lo, I am about to create new heavens and a new earth;
The things of the past shall not be remembered or come to mind.
Instead, there shall always be rejoicing and happiness in what I create.

—ISAIAH 65:17–18

The Angels of the Cosmos are called the Regulative Choirs of Angels, for they have the assignment of governing the entire cosmos, including all the galaxies. The Angels of the Cosmos are the Dominions, the Powers, and the Virtues, in descending levels of power and authority. (The classification of the ranks of the

Angels of the Cosmos is not universally accepted by the angelic scholars of the ages.)[1] Their assignment is quite beyond the scope of the human intellect in these times, since they mediate the power and control of the universe and all its galaxies. The planet Earth is only a small speck in the cosmos.

The highest of the Angels of the Cosmos dwell in the Choir known as Dominions, though some have referred to them as Dominations. The power of the Dominion Choir is so vast that it transcends the human imagination. All leadership over created matter emanates from the Dominions, who receive their power and assignments directly from the Thrones. Their power is then mediated from the Dominions to the lesser Choirs of angels over the entire cosmos, including the planet Earth. The Dominions represent exquisite order and the discipline of order. The law of perfect cause and effect flows through them to all creation.

Dominions are angels of leadership. They dispense to the lower Choirs of Angels, who travel about the cosmos and the world showing people the proper things to do and the attitudes to preserve in order to be happy. Those who be-friend the Dominion Choir of Angels and who allow their Guardian Angel to access their power level have no difficulty making correct decisions. They have fulfilling and prosperous relationships. They enjoy their lives immensely. They are "natural" leaders, for all authentic leadership resides in God and is mediated according to His Will.

The Dominions are known as Spirits of Wisdom. The Prophet Isaiah calls wisdom the highest of the gifts of the Holy Spirit of Love. Understanding, counsel, fortitude, knowledge, godliness, and fear of the Lord flow from the gift of wisdom. Those who bear the favor and protection of the Dominion Choir of Angels draw near to the Holy Spirit of Love and experience a profusion of those gifts.

All angels, but especially the Dominions, are filled with wisdom. Their assignment is the universe in which we dwell. They mediate perfectly the Holy Spirit of Love. They long to communicate the Holy Spirit of Love to us.

Those who have befriended the powerful Dominion Choir of Angels may not see these Angels of Leadership, but they constantly experience their effects. Living replicas of Divine Beauty, the Dominion angels are filled with zeal for the splendor and order of creation.

The Dominions greatly transcend the sovereignty of the lesser Choirs of Angels, who are subject to them in obedience.[2] Their love is a powerful tool when we invite them to lead with us in our tasks and assignments. The more significant the assignment, the more that is needed of the graciousness, wisdom, and power of God that resides in the Dominion Choir of Angels.

The Dominions, as bearers of Divine Wisdom and the gifts of the Holy Spirit, are great Ministers of God's Justice to the cosmos and the world. They govern the forces of chaos, especially unruly passions. The Dominions receive their instructions directly from the Thrones, who dwell in the very presence of God. For that reason Dominions are far above the Powers and Virtues, who may approach the Dominions only at their beckon.[3] The mediated guidance of the entire Angelic Court is a mystery of God's Graciousness.

No angel will ever be a coconspirator in any endeavor that lacks Truth.[4] Those who disavow Truth lose all angelic protection. Angels help us only to obey God's Will. When we disobey God's Will for us, we bring suffering upon ourselves. Such is the perfect law of justice. Since angels are empowered to chastise those who disobey God, it is wise to take seriously the great Commandments of the Creator. If Angel Power has been severed by an unkind or untruthful act, it requires sincere, heartfelt repentance to restore it. The angels make obedience to God's Will a journey of joy.

Nations and people are quite comfortable in positions of responsibility and authority when they are under the protection of the Dominion Choir of Angels. No personal agenda or ego is involved. Rather all action is dedicated to the glory of God through perfect obedience to His Divine Will. It is impossible to know and obey the perfect will of God without Angel Power.

Powers

The Powers are ranked second among the Angels of the Cosmos by Saint Thomas Aquinas. They are recognized as special Warrior Angels against evil. They defend the cosmos, including humans, against evil. The Powers particularly watch over and come to the assistance of those who govern countries, cities, congregations, and agencies. They are tireless defenders of goodness. They are so intelligent that they can detect schemes and tricks before they happen. They always send warnings to us when others seek to hurt us. Survival requires that, through the mercy of God, we hear their voices. They speak only in silence.

The love and light of God bathes all creation in His Warmth and Protection. The only known exception is evil and its realms, which are devoid of the presence of God. Saint Paul warned that there are evil forces that wreak havoc in the cosmos. He indicated that the real battle is with unseen forces: "For our struggle is not with flesh and blood, but with the principalities, with the powers, with the world rulers of this present darkness, with the evil spirits in the heavens" (Ephesians 6:12).

Saint Paul recognized that there are evil spirits who formerly were members of the Powers Choir. Such demons possess hideous malevolence, which they spew to pillage and destroy. These fallen angels of the Powers class should be relatively easy to spot since they bear pure evil in their essence, but they are quite cunning. Their lust is for raw power and greatness. They have used their blessings to exalt themselves, rebelling against God's Plan and Authority. Their blessings have become curses. They are filled with hubris. They shovel illusionary power and sick, empty prestige upon the aspirations of God's People on the earth. Their influence manifests itself in concentration camps, rape camps, and all heinous expressions of cruelty and malfeasance.

Evil forces are being unmasked. Great and holy leadership is rooted in God and mediated by the Angelic Choirs. The Thrones constantly distribute the very power of God to the Dominions, and the Dominions fill the Powers with the might of God's Omnipotence.

God's Holy Angels are more powerful than all the evil in creation. The demons crave darkness. As evil forces are exposed to the light of Truth, humans are freed of their presence. One angel alone is strong enough to destroy all the

evil in the world, for any one angel may call upon the entire Nine Choirs of Angels. However, angels are most humble. They do not interfere where they are not invited.

Wisdom leads people to ask angels to defend their home, their city, their country, the planet. Those who love invite angels to protect their family. Angel Power is a gracious gift from God. Angels help us to live in their own splendor of love and peace and joy. They await an invitation to participate in our home life, our village and city life, our national and international life. When everyone is prepared to invite holy angels into their lives and decisions, the earth will be a gracious, hospitable land of delight. Those who ask receive Angel Power.

Virtues

Angel Virtues, the lowest-ranking Angels of the Cosmos, are exquisitely strong angels. They are known as Spirits of Motion. They have control over all the elements.[5] The winds and the rain, the ice and the snow, the stars and the moon, and even the sun are subject to their command. The Virtues govern all of nature. They have great love for us. They watch over us most tenderly. Their special job is to help us to grow in holiness and to avoid accidents. They are so strong that they can order a comet to stop falling.

On facing page: The Virtues govern all of nature. The Blessed Virgin Mary ascends to the highest ranks of virtue.

The Virtue Angels are well known because of the miracles that flow from their presence. They bring about the signs and wonders that humans crave. When the great cosmic miracle of the spinning sun thrilled and terrified seventy thousand eyewitnesses at Fatima, Portugal, in 1917, assuredly the Virtues were performing their feats. Great scientists with extraordinary discoveries owe their gifts to the light of the Virtues. The mighty athletes whose feats of physical skill thrill the imaginations of normal mortals are aided by the Virtue Choir of Angels. Writers and teachers, artists and musicians, are beloved beneficiaries of the Virtues.

The angels of the Virtue Choir receive their power and authority from the Powers. Though the Virtues bring the signs and wonders to the cosmos, the earth, and its people, it is the Powers who contain the signs and wonders. The Powers must restrain the Virtues so that they do not tempt humans to pride by their generosity as they present the gifts of the Angels of the Cosmos to the people of the earth.[6] Special envoys of God bringing His Miracles to the cosmos and to the people of the earth, the Angels of the Cosmos do all for His Glory and the well-being of all God's People.

Most people all over the world know about miracles. Almost everyone's family has experienced a miracle somewhere along the path of its history. The Virtue Angels are in charge of dispensing miracles. They make wonderful advocates for us with the higher Choirs of Angels.

Those who access the Virtues never want. They are able to obtain miracles when they are most needed, so long as the miracles do not interfere with God's Will.[7] Those who ask the Virtues to intercede for them frequently experience delightful surprises.

A young mother was at the airport. Her plane was scheduled to depart within the hour. Suddenly an overwhelming desire forced her to rush outside, hail a cab, and return to her home. At the top of the stairs in the entry sat her six-year-old daughter. "Oh, Mama, I knew you would come! I sent my Guardian Angel to get you!" cried the ecstatic child as she clung to her mother's neck. Many kisses later, amid reassurances of the presence of angels, the child was gently tucked into bed with her heart filled with gratitude. The mother returned to the airport certain that her plane would be waiting. The angels are kind. Her seat had been upgraded to first class, and the flight was boarding as she approached the gate.

The Virtues help us when we are sick or alone or frightened. These angels have the power to make difficult things easy. Agents of Almighty God, they perform His Great Miracles every day, more than all the stars in the sky. And who can count the stars in the sky! When the Virtues are our special angelic friends, they have many gifts of illumination for us each moment that we look.

George Washington and Angel Power at Valley Forge, 1777

On the North American continent the thirteen colonies were engaged in a fierce battle to gain independence from corrupt rule. General George Washington was the commander-in-chief of the pitiful, struggling colonial army. His soldiers were ragged. They were starving. They had nothing to keep them warm in the bitter winter of 1777 except the fire of love in their hearts for their families and the dreams for the infant nation they cherished. These brave visionaries faced inhuman odds as the battle of Valley Forge loomed. It was then that their faith-filled commander-in-chief, in full view of his troops, knelt in the snow to implore that the blessings and Providence of Almighty God be bestowed upon the dedicated men, who carried the hopes and aspirations of freedom in their hearts.

General George Washington experienced an apparition of a Beautiful Lady clothed with the sun, who appeared to him during those dark days of starvation and defeat at Valley Forge, Pennsylvania. Mysterious and unidentified, she appeared to George Washington to encourage him, guide him, and offer warnings about the future of the country that had been entrusted to God through the Immaculate Heart of Mary one year earlier by the first Bishop of the thirteen colonies, Jesuit John Carroll.

A colleague of George Washington and an eyewitness of the event, Anthony Sherman, recounted the story of Wesley Bradshaw. This oral history of George Washington's mysterious apparition at the time of the American Revolution was originally published in the *National Tribune*, December 1880.

> "George Washington . . . would hardly have been the type of man one would expect to be seeking visionary manifestations, or easily be taken in by them. From the opening of the [American] Revolution we experienced all phases of fortune, now

good and now ill, one time victorious and another time conquered. The darkest period we had, I think, was when Washington, after several reverses, retreated to Valley Forge, where
he resolved to pass the winter of 1777. Ah! I have often seen
the tears course down our dear commander's careworn cheeks,
as he would be conversing with confidential officers about the
condition of his poor soldiers. You have doubtless heard the
story of Washington going to the thicket to pray. It was not
only true but he used often to pray in secret for aid and comfort
from God, the Interposition of whose Divine Providence
brought us safely through the darkest days of tribulation.

"One day, I remember it well, the chilly wind whistled
through the leafless trees, though the sky was cloudless and the
sun shone brightly. He remained in his quarters nearly all afternoon alone. When he came out I noticed that his face was a
shade paler than usual, and there seemed to be something on his
mind of more than ordinary importance. Returning just after
dark, he dispatched an orderly to the quarters of another officer,
who was presently in attendance. After a preliminary conversa-
tion of about half an hour, Washington, gazing upon us with that
strange look of dignity, which he alone could command, said:

" 'I do not know whether it is owing to the anxiety of
my mind, but this afternoon, as I was sitting at this table engaged in preparing a dispatch, something disturbed me. Look-

ing up, I saw standing opposite a singularly beautiful female. So astonished was I, for I had given strict orders not to be disturbed, that it was some moments before I found language to inquire the purpose of her presence. A second, third, even a fourth time did I repeat my question but received no answer from my mysterious visitor, except a slight raising of her eyes. By this time I felt strange sensations spreading through me. I would have risen but the riveted gaze of the being before me rendered volition impossible. I essayed once more to address her, but my tongue had become useless. Even thought itself had become paralyzed. A new influence, mysterious, potent, irresistible, took possession of me. All I could do was to gaze steadily, at my unknown visitor. Gradually the surrounding atmosphere filled with sensation and grew luminous. Everything about me seemed to rarefy, the mysterious visitor herself becoming more airy and yet more distinct to my sight than before. I now began to feel as one dying, or rather to experience the sensation which I have sometimes imagined accompanies dissolution. I did not think, I did not reason, I did not move. All, alike, were impossible. I was conscious only of gazing fixedly at my companion. Presently I heard a voice say,

"Son of the Republic, look and learn!"

while at the same time my visitor extended her arm eastward. I looked and beheld a heavy white vapor rising, at some distance, fold upon fold. This gradually dissipated and I watched before me lay spread out in one vast plain all the countries of the world: Europe, Asia, Africa and America. I saw rolling and tossing between Europe and America, the billows of the Atlantic Ocean, and between America and Asia lay the Pacific.

"Son of the Republic," said the mysterious voice as before, ***"look and learn."***

" 'At that moment I beheld a dark shadowy being, standing, or rather floating in mid-air between Europe and America. Dipping water out of the ocean with his right hand, he cast it upon America, while that in his left hand went upon the European countries. Immediately a cloud arose from these countries, and joined in mid-ocean. For a while it remained stationary, and then it moved slowly westward, until it enveloped America in its folds. Sharp flashes of lightning gleamed through at intervals; and I heard the smothered groans of the American people. A second time the angel dipped water from the ocean and sprinkled it as before. The dark cloud was then drawn back to the ocean, in whose heaving bellows it sank from view. A third time I heard the mysterious voice say:

"Son of the Republic, look and learn."

" 'I cast my eyes upon America and beheld villages, towns and cities springing up one after another until the whole land, from the Atlantic to the Pacific, was dotted with them. Again I heard the voice say,

"Son of the Republic, the end of the century comes. Look and learn."

And with this the dark, shadowy angel turned its face southward, and from Africa an ill-omened spectra approached our land. It flitted slowly over every town and city of the land. The inhabitants presently set themselves in battle array against each other.

" 'As I continued to look I saw a bright angel, on whose brow rested a crown of light on which was traced the word UNION, place an American flag between the divided nation and say:

"Remember ye are brethren."

Instantly the inhabitants, casting from them weapons, became friends once more and united around the National Standard. Again I heard the voice of my most beautiful and mysterious visitor say,

"Son of the Republic, look and learn."

At this, the dark shadowy angel placed a trumpet to his mouth and blew three distinct blasts; and taking water from the ocean he sprinkled it upon Europe, Asia and Africa.

" 'Then my eyes beheld a fearful scene: from each of these countries arose thick black clouds that were soon joined into one. Throughout this mass there gleamed a bright Red Light, by which I saw hordes of armed men, who, moving with the cloud, marched by land and sailed by sea to America which country was enveloped in the volume of cloud.

" 'And I saw these vast armies devastate the whole country and burn the villages, towns and cities that I saw springing up. As my ears listened to the thundering of the cannon, the clashing of the swords, and the shouts and cries of millions in mortal combat, I again heard the mysterious voice say:

"Son of the Republic, look and learn."

As the voice ceased, the bright angel, for the last time, dipped water from the ocean and sprinkled it upon America. Instantly the dark cloud rolled back, together with the armies it had brought, leaving the inhabitants of the land victorious. Once more I beheld villages, towns and cities springing up where I had seen them before; while the bright angel, planting the azure standard he had brought in the middle of them, cried in a loud voice,

"While the stars remain and the heavens send down dew upon the earth, so long shall the Union last."

" 'And taking from her angelic brow the crown on which was blazoned the word UNION, she placed it upon the National Standard, while people kneeling down, said, Amen.

" 'The scene instantly began to fade away, and I saw nothing but the rising, curling vapor I had first beheld. This also disappeared and I found myself once more gazing upon the mysterious beautiful visitor who said,

"Son of the Republic, what you have seen is thus: three great perils will come upon the Republic. The most fearful is the third, but the whole world united shall not prevail upon her. Let every child of the Republic learn to live for God, His land and the Union."

" 'With these words the beautiful visitor and the bright angel accompanying her disappeared from my sight.'

"Such, my friend, were the very words I heard from

Washington's own lips and America will do well to profit by them," concluded the narrator of this Oral History.[8]

The Declaration of Independence of the thirteen original colonies was a turning point in the history of humankind, for it augured government rooted in sensitivity to Divine Truth. The United States of America was founded as a "City Upon the Hill." The Declaration of Independence, which inspired the Constitution of the United States of America, was earned by George Washington and his poor, starving troops at Valley Forge. It created a blueprint for moral government that had never before entered the consciousness of nations. Valley Forge was the turning point of the American Revolution.

Only God knows the identity of the Beautiful Lady of George Washington's apparition. Some think she is the Blessed Virgin Mary, who appeared as Queen of the Angels in response to the consecration one year earlier that entrusted all of the Americas and the Philippines to the special care of her Immaculate Heart. Certainly the Beautiful Lady had angels in her retinue. General Washington spoke of a "bright angel with a crown of light" who responded to the directions of the Beautiful Lady, so it is clear that the Beautiful Lady outranked the bright angel.

Others believe the Beautiful Lady may have been a Dominion in corporeal form. The mission of the Beautiful Lady falls within the responsibilities of the Dominion Choir. The bright angel may have been from the Powers or the Principalities. The three Choirs of Angels of the cosmos bear the authority and power that corresponded to General Washington's requests.

The leader of each family, village, city, state, and nation has a particular Guardian Angel to watch over and guide his or her decisions as they affect the place wherein his or her authority is vested. Such Guardian Angel has direct access to the Choirs of the Angels of the Cosmos. Every juridical leader, not only of places but also of groups such as schools, hospitals, churches, businesses, laboratories, and organizations, has a particular Guardian Angel who guards and guides. Because the angels are steeped in humility and restrained by human freedom of choice, they will not interfere in human affairs unless it is the direct will of God or unless they are properly invited.

Many leaders of nations and families have entrusted their fate to the Queen of Angels and her entire Celestial Court. The United States is one such nation. England, the home of Washington's forebears, is known as "Mary's Dowry" because of its ancient consecration to the Blessed Mother by the English King and ranking Archbishop. France, Portugal, Spain, and other nations, too, are similarly consecrated. Apparently God takes consecrations seriously.

The message of the Beautiful Lady to General Washington is poignant today for all people on earth, even as it was in 1777 for the thirteen colonies:

Remember, you are brothers and sisters.

The United States, like all nations, has a personal Guardian Angel assigned to guard and guide the country. Perhaps the Beautiful Lady of Washington's apparition is the Guardian Angel of the United States. She could be from any of the Nine Choirs. The destiny of the United States is intimately related to its Guardian Angel, as is the destiny of each nation.

The Angels of the Cosmos mediate the power for order and goodness to the earth. Guardian Angels, bearing highly specialized gifts, are the divinely appointed liaisons who personally stand guard and guide each nation on earth. Obviously Guardian Angels of some nations are kept much busier than others. The work of the Guardian Angels of nations depends largely upon the leadership and faith of the constituent peoples. Each town, village, and hamlet also has a special, divinely appointed Guardian Angel. The power of the nation for goodness depends upon the condition of the hearts of those who are governed. Goodness begets goodness. Angel Power begets Angel Power.

One day every village, town, city, state, and nation, and every home, school, office, factory, hospital, ship, plane, airport, and public meeting place will have a special shrine acknowledging the presence of its personal Guardian Angel. Some shrines will be a mere corner in a room where two or more pause to silently address the invisible angel spirit of love who dwells there. Other shrines of the Guardian Angel will be grand, and thousands upon thousands will gather there to celebrate the generosity and love of God with the Guardian Angel and all the Angels of the Nine Choirs.

The brilliantly humble angels are empowered to light and guard, rule and guide as the inhabitants of places learn to access Angel Power. As holy Angel Power is more widely understood and accessed, angels and humans acknowledge that they are brothers and sisters in God. In that glorious light the planet Earth becomes God's Holy House of Prayer, which is the Kingdom of Heaven.

Meditation

I command firm moral leadership.

When you reward sinful behavior, you provoke My Wrath.

When you reward sinful behavior, you are not My children.

When you reward sinful behavior, you are Satan's accomplice.

I do not bless the tree that produces fruit to serve Satan's calls.

Those who do not obey My Commandments do not love Me.

Those who do not love Me do not honor Me.

I do not honor those who do not honor Me.

Today I serve those who love Me and those who do not love Me alike.

Those who love Me keep My Commandments.

My Father and I come and dwell in those who keep My
*   Commandments.*

Soon where We do not dwell there will be no life.

You will know those who love Me and honor Me by the fire of love
*   in their hearts.*

Where there is no love, there is no life.

Love begets love. Justice begets justice. Sin begets sin.

On facing page: The Guardian Angel of the United States

Prayer

TO THE GUARDIAN ANGEL OF THE UNITED STATES

(OR ANY OTHER NATION)

O glorious Guardian Angel of the United States

You bear the great and blessed privilege of protecting the land
of our hopes and dreams.

We turn to you o angel of God, great bearer of His justice and
beauty and truth.

Guide our decision. Guard our goals. Purify our appetites.

Bring the light of God's mercy to our people.

Bring the bounty of God's mercy to our people.

Bring the love of God's mercy to our people.

Rescue us o great angel of God's justice from the mistakes of
our past.

Ennoble all our people with the truth of God's will.

Strengthen all our people with the wisdom of God's will.

Endow all our people with the blessings of God's will.

Send the generosity of God's Spirit upon our lands and rivers
and streams.

Carry the graciousness of God's Holiness to the winds in our
  trees and flowers and mountains and plains.
Bless our animals and fishes and birds.
Lift all our people on the wings of your might and fly with us
  into the Heart of God's Mercy forever.
Amen.

Chapter Twelve

Angels of the World: Principalities, Archangels, and Angels

At that time there shall arise
Michael, the great prince,
guardian of your people;
It shall be a time unsurpassed in distress
since nations began until that time.
At that time your people shall escape,
everyone who is found written in the book.
Many of those who sleep in the dust of the earth
shall awake;

some shall live forever,

others shall be an everlasting horror and disgrace.

But the wise shall shine brightly like the splendor of the firmament,

And those who lead the many to justice shall be like the stars

> *forever.*

—DANIEL 12:1–3

The remaining three Choirs of Angels are Angels of the World. They are assigned to the planet Earth. They are called the Administrative Angels because they carry out the directions of the Angels of the Cosmos, who are the Regulative Angels.

Principalities

The Angel Principalities are the highest-ranking Angels of the World. They are Administrative Angels. It is not known how many of them there are, but each nation, city, province, town, village, and hamlet has a special Angel Principality whose job it is to guard and guide that particular place along with the Guardian Angel assigned to that place. It is probable that the Guardian Angel of a place would be from the Angelic Choir that most closely resembles the location's destiny. An example may be the Guardian Angel of Mount Athos. High in the mountains, on the coast of Greece, this holy monastery that fosters pure contemplation as a way of life may be guarded by a Seraph or a Cherub along with the Principality assigned to the property.[1]

There are countless numbers of Principalities. Throughout the centuries, some experts have referred to them as Princes because they are believed to specifically be in charge of nations, countries, regions, cities, places, and communities. Their influence upon human beings occurs in many ways. They communicate ideas, stir up circumstances, and even interfere in human affairs to accomplish the direct will of God. It is in the area of the indirect will of God that these angel Principalities are empowered by human behavior to influence the life-style of those who inhabit their sphere of influence.[2]

The Principalities have jurisdiction over those who govern people and places. The wisdom of these angels guides events to bring blessings of contentment and abundance to the places they protect.

Human disrespect, indifference, and disobedience drive divine protection away from human pursuits.[3] When the angels are not protecting humans, many terrible things can and do happen. Angel Power is centered on Divine Protection. The Principalities are in constant attendance, on duty at their place of assignment despite the attitude and behavior of the people who dwell there. The Principalities have at their disposal all the gifts, weapons, powers, and authority of the entire Angelic Court for the protection and well-being of their particular assignment. It is up to the people to recognize and access the presence of angels. Much is expected of those to whom much is given.

Justice is embroidered into the substance of creation. God intends that humans reap what they sow. The Angel Principalities may use only the authority that the people who inhabit their location allow them. As the faith of people all over the world increases, Angel Power solves the problems that human limitations create on earth. It takes human virtue to recognize an invisible angel's presence. But the angels are pure virtue. Angels and humans are a divinely blessed combination.

Guangzhou, the capital of Guangdong Province in South China, is an important industrial and foreign trade center. According to legends the locals tell, the city was founded by five angels. Each angel came down from Heaven astride a goat, and each goat held a stalk of rice in its mouth, symbolizing God's favor upon the region. It is believed that the area will never suffer from famine. The region is said to be seriously evaluating the implementation of human rights and economic reforms. Is someone accessing Angel Power in Guangzhou?

The angels' luminous swords of goodness shine in the sky above all people on earth. Would that normal, caring people in every country allow the Principalities to help that country's people have a good and prosperous life. Does your community invite the Good Angels to dwell with you? Why don't you invite them? Only you and the angels need know.

Archangels

The Archangels are the special emissaries of the Principalities. They transmit to us the good intentions that the Angel Virtues bring from the Powers. The Archangels have a most special and protective love for all the people of the earth. They personally intervene in crises and times of need to protect and guard nations, cities, airports, churches, houses, and families. They always bring great goodness and much happiness to those who invoke their aid. They bring peace, prosperity, unity, joy, abundance, graciousness, kindness, gentleness, humility, and love to those who are dedicated to Truth.

You know the great Archangel Saint Michael and some of his mighty deeds. Many people throughout the centuries have claimed to have been spared terrible death on the battlefield by Saint Michael and the Archangels. History books are filled with wonderful stories and paintings of the miracles of Saint Michael the Archangel.

In a single second an Archangel can travel from one end of the universe to the other. Any angel can be in many places at one time, even though the places are millions of miles apart. Try to imagine the light of the sun. It, too, can be in many places at one time without diminishing any of its power. So it is with the angels because they carry the power of God. "An angel is in a place in so far as it exercises its powers there and not elsewhere."[4] It can cease to apply its powers there and begin to apply them elsewhere.

Every generation of people from the beginning has had personal experiences with the Archangels. Most families have special stories of the Archangels in their own history, and each nation, too, has its own special Archangel.

Those nations whose people pray enjoy the bounty of holy Angel Power and are safe from the power of the rebel spirits, who bring darkness, poverty, famine, hatred, suspicion, division, violence, and cruel death.

Angels

The Angels have a wonderful job. Though they are the lowest-ranking angels in the Angelic Court, they have the capacity to access any and all the other angels at any time. The Angels are most caring and solicitous to assist those who ask for their help. The Acts of the Apostles is filled with stories of the angelic intervention of the angels in the lives of the early Church.[5] Each Angel carries the power of the entire Celestial Court.

Angels are exquisitely powerful in comparison to human beings. Martin Luther had great devotion to Angels, referring to them as spiritual creatures created by God for the service of Christendom and the Church.[6]

The followers of Muhammad are extolled to revere Angels. The Koran addresses their duties toward holy angels: "The existence of Angels and their purity are absolutely required to be believed in the Koran: and he is reckoned an infidel who denies there are such beings, or hates any of them."[7]

Though we rarely see Angels, if at all, everyone experiences their effects. They are invisible spirits of sheer intelligence and will. Saint Thomas Aquinas had an angelic apparition and afterward spoke of an Angel as "The most excellent of creatures because he bears the strongest resemblance to God." An Angel is able to penetrate the most secret complexities of science in an instant.

The Old Testament recounts the kindness and compassion of the Angels toward humans: An Angel brought food to Daniel in the lion's den (Daniel 14:33–39). Saint Raphael the Archangel appeared in human form to accompany Tobias's son on a journey. Along the way the Archangel found him safety, employment, and even a beautiful wife (Tobit 12:19–20).

The Fourth Lateran Council has decreed the existence of Angels as an article of faith. The voices of the Angels constantly praise the goodness and kindness of God. Psalm 103 extols the glory of the Angels and of God's children too:

> Bless the LORD, all you angels, mighty in strength and
>   attentive, obedient to every command.
> Bless the LORD, all you hosts, ministers who do God's will.
> Bless the LORD, all creatures, everywhere in God's domain.
> Bless the LORD, my soul!—Psalms 103:21–22

Angels in Dying and Death

Many years ago, in a small town, an old man lay dying. His family gathered near to pray. Suddenly the room was flooded with immense light, and the scent of fresh roses filled the air. Everyone saw a group of angels surround the old man. Then darkness filled the room. The family was preparing to leave, but two angels came back, approached the body of the old man, and reverently kissed his forehead. The youngest child present heard the words

> *"He never once made us ashamed before the Throne of the Great God of Abraham, Isaac, and Jacob!"*

Angels are quite powerful and indispensable at the hour of death, not only for the dying person but also for those involved in the death. As death approaches, the final battle for a human soul takes place. Because we die as we live, Angels are indispensable during every human lifetime. Origen, the third-century church scholar, describes it this way:

> A great [heavenly] multitude is assembled to watch you when you combat. . . . It is as if we said that thousands gather to watch a contest in which contestants of outstanding reputation are engaged. When you are engaged in the conflict you can say with Saint Paul: "We are made a spectacle to the world and to angels and to men." The whole world, therefore, all the angels on the right and on the left, all men, both those on the side of God and the others—all will hear us fighting the fight for Christianity.—The angels in heaven will rejoice with us.[8]

Since we do not know the day or the hour of our final encounter with darkness, those who have accessed Angel Power throughout their lives can hope to be like Lazarus, who in the New Testament is described being ". . . carried by the angels to the bosom of Abraham" (Luke 16:22). In the Epistle of Jude, Saint Michael the Archangel is shown battling with the devil over the body of Moses. Saint Chrysostom said:

> "If we need a guide in passing from one city to another, how much more will the soul need someone to point out the way when it breaks the bonds of flesh and passes on to the future life."[9]

Moses was so special in his obedience and faithfulness to God that the evil spirits could not resist one last effort to ensnare his earthly remains. The holy angels however, always come to serve the saints. That is one of their assignments. Angel Power flows to every person on the earth who has at least one personal, invisible spirit of pure love, a Guardian Angel who stays with us from the moment God breathes us out of His Heart until our natural death.

Many people throughout history who have been quite sick have told us that they have seen their Guardian Angel. They explain the beauty and love and peace that their own dear Guardian Angel shares with them.

MESSAGE FROM A GUARDIAN ANGEL

You are well my beloved friend.
You are God's treasure.
Can't you see me now?
Ah, you still harbor some fear?
It covers lack of faith, lack of trust.
Pray for strong faith, for hope.
When these virtues join the love in your heart you will be whole.

Those among the sick who have experienced their Guardian Angel speak of the beauty and love and peace that their own dear Guardian Angel has shared with them. Because it is not yet time to go to the land of the Angels, the sick people get well and tell us about the Lord, the Blessed Mother, the Saints,

the Prophets, and beautiful Guardian Angels who watch over each of us. Those who access Angel Power have no terror of the Unknown. They see with angel eyes and hear with angel ears.

The path to death is lined with Angels. The path is beautiful for those who know their Guardian Angel well.

SONG OF THE GUARDIAN ANGEL

Be at peace, dear precious friend.
You have nothing to fear. You belong to God.
I shall cradle you in my arms and sing you gentle songs.
I shall teach you to play.
I will give you toys of such immense beauty that your heart will sing
  before the Trinity as a clear bell calling all God's Lost children
  to the throne of God, their Father, for the last time.
I shall sing with you. I will love with you. I will die with you.
Be at peace, my dear precious friend.
I am always with you.
Peace. Peace. Peace.

The wisdom of the ages has given humanity Angelology, the science of Angels. It teaches that:

- Angels assist our soul to escape the sufferings of death
- Our Guardian Angel accompanies us and assures a peaceful journey for us

• Our Guardian Angel, accessing any and all the Angel Power we may need from the Nine Choirs of Angels, defends our passage from this life to the next from the demons who line the path of exit

• Our Guardian Angel introduces us to the angels in charge of the Gate of Heaven—the fiery Cherubim, who bear the great Sword of Justice

• If our soul is not totally pure but we are repentant, our soul must be purified before we may proceed into the immediate presence of God

• We must undergo a baptism of the fire of purification, which is administered by Angels.[10]

Throughout the centuries the process has been articulated in the following way:

> [After natural death] the Nine Choirs of Angels is our witness, the Powers of Heaven are waiting for us lovingly, to see when and in what manner we return from this battle, how many spoils we have carried off. They watch with attention, they make a most thorough search to see which of us are carrying the greatest quantity of gold [of charity] or silver [of charity] or precious stone [of charity]. . . . There will be a thorough search when we arrive there, to discover what each of us is bringing; and according to the measure of what each one has brought . . . will be determined the dwelling that he deserves.[11]

Once the admittance procedures to Heaven are completed, we meet all those who have been waiting for us who are already in Heaven. There is extraordinary rejoicing and sharing. Tradition teaches that the faithful receive a great reception in Heaven. Scripture refers to the celebration as "The Wedding Feast of the Lamb" where God the Father welcomes His Precious children home.

SONG OF THE ETERNAL FATHER

See Me in the world, My children.

*Experience My Immense, Unfathomable Love for each redeemed child
    of Mine.*

I am your true Father, your source, your life.

I love what I create. I love you, My Dear children.

When you call to Me, I respond.

*Woe to you, dear little ones of Mine, who do not call to Me, for I am
    humble.*

*When you turn from Me, My Little Ones, I call you again and
    again.*

I lure you. I woo you.

*My Heart dies of abandonment, as My Beloved Jesus showed all of
    you, when My little ones run from Me.*

I have made you free, little ones, free to choose Me or to deny Me.

When you refuse Me, My Beloved children, you choose death.

While there is time, call to Me. Come to Me.

Persevere in Me, in My Ways, o beautiful children of Mine.

Soon we shall all make merry at the Wedding Feast of the Lamb.

O My Little children, how beautiful you are!

How pleased I am with your preparations.

Thousands and thousands prepare night and day.

Each prayer is an ornament at the feast.

Each renounced appetite of the world is a garment of such splendor
 that My children shall exalt forever at its sight.

Little ones, pray now and fast now.

Persevere, My Little Ones.

You are Mine.

Angel Power from the Beyond

Many believe that little babies and old, old people, can actually see their Guardian Angels.

Mary Joy was born on October 2nd after a long and difficult delivery that included an emergency cesarean section for her mother. Mary Joy's daddy said she was the most beautiful baby who ever was. The infant seemed to understand. She smiled and slept and awoke to smile some more.

Those who saw her said there was something unique and quite special about Mary Joy. She was filled with peace and love. Her grandfather could not stop looking at her. Fascinated, he often wondered, "Is this baby seeing the angels?" An aura of light seemed to surround her. From time to time there was a faint aroma of incense around the tiny bassinet. A sacred presence sometimes seemed to hover about the room. Mary Joy's radiance was obvious to all.

One day Mary Joy's grandfather confided, "Mama and I often talked about the Guardian Angels." Taking his daughter's hand gently in his, he quietly mused, "I seem to remember that when you were an infant, Mama said you were seeing the angels."

Startled, the new young mother blurted, "Mama and three angels came to be with me in the labor room at the hospital. Mama told me I would not die and that my baby would always have the special protection of the angels. When Mama kissed me, I knew everything would be all right. The angels told me my baby's name is Mary Joy in honor of their Queen. They said the Blessed Mother is the joy of the angels."

Grandpa was crying now. "I have missed your grandma so much, little lady," he said as he bent down and kissed Mary Joy. "Please ask the Angels to come for me soon and bring me to your grandma." He felt his loneliness melt in the tiny infant's smile as he experienced the joy of love rooted in hope once again.

The immense love and beauty and power of the Angels is beyond the capacity of the human mind to fathom. Someday when we least expect it, we will see Angels.

Angels escort us into Paradise. Those who have cultivated a deep, loving relationship with the Angels enjoy a reciprocity of trust that eliminates all fear, anxiety, worry.

Origen realized the following: "When this tabernacle [our body] has been dissolved, and we have begun to enter into the Holies [the spirit world of the Angels] and pass on to the Promised Land (Paradise), those who are really holy and whose place is in the Holy of Holies [union with God] will make their way supported by the angels."[12]

Saint Paul brought light to the mystery of the last days when he said, "Then we who are alive, who are left, shall be caught up together with them [the Angels] in the clouds to meet the Lord in the air" (1 Thessalonians 4:17). Long ago Eusebius foresaw that "The angels will lead the elect to their blessed end, when they will be lifted up, carried as was Elias on an angelic chariot, amid the rays of heavenly light."[13]

All the Angels in the Nine Choirs see and hear everything that occurs on earth and the heavens. They love us with God's Pure Love. Their job is to facilitate our journey on earth so that it is joyous and abundant as we prepare to take our places in the triumphant Nine Choirs of God's Glory. Angels have the power to make our lives a mosaic of peace, happiness, and real love. We have the power to access Angels.

The Angels carry our dreams, goals, and longings with us and often for us. The Angels are our first, best, and last friends. With their presence, assistance, and wisdom, all that is not well becomes well. We die as we live.

Meditation

"Strive for peace with everyone, and for that holiness without which no one will see the Lord."   —HEBREWS 12:14

"There is no god higher than truth."

—MAHATMA GANDHI AS QUOTED IN

TRUE PATRIOTISM: SOME

SAYINGS OF MAHATMA GANDHI,

1939. EDITED BY S. HOBHOUSE

"Peace comes from within. Do not seek it without."

—BUDDHA

"And when a man injures and oppresses you and deals unjustly with you, you should deal kindly with him and forgive him. Thus you will strike at the root of hatred and enmity and he who is your enemy will become your friend."   —HOLY KORAN 41:34

"The reward of humility and fear of the Lord is riches, honor and life."   —PROVERBS 22:4

Prayer

Guardian Angel of mine
Given to me by God's love,
Teach me all the secrets of Heaven.
Sing to me of the beauty of your world.
Protect me each moment that I live.
Carry me in your arms
On the wings of God's loving power
Till at last I see your glorious face forever.
Amen.

Part IV

How to Access the Power of Angels

I am convinced that neither death, nor life, nor angels, nor principalities, nor present things, nor future things, nor powers, nor height, nor depth, nor any creature will be able to separate us from the love of God in Christ Jesus our Lord.

—ROMANS 8:38–39

Chapter Thirteen

Angel Power in
Tragedy and Dreams

❖

*Pray that this does not happen in winter. For those times will have
tribulation such as has not been since the beginning of God's creation
until now, nor ever will be. If the Lord had not shortened those days,
no one would be saved; but for the sake of the elect whom he chose,
he did shorten the days. If anyone says to you then, "Look, here is
the Messiah! Look, there he is!" do not believe it. False messiahs
and false prophets will arise and will perform signs and wonders in
order to mislead, if that were possible, the elect. Be watchful! I have
told it all to you beforehand.*

But in those days after that tribulation

the sun will be darkened, and the moon will not give its light,

and the stars will be falling from the sky,

and the powers in the heavens will be shaken.

And then they will see 'the Son of Man coming in the clouds'
with great power and glory, and then he will send out the angels and
gather [his] elect from the four winds, from the end of the earth to
the end of the sky. . . .

Heaven and earth will pass away, but my words will not pass
away. But of that day or hour, no one knows, neither the angels in
heaven, nor the Son, but only the Father. Be watchful! Be alert!
You do not know when the time will come.

—MARK 13:18–33

More often than we like, tragedy strikes with no warning or explanation. Who decides those who survive a plane crash? Why do some languish in intensive care units while others walk away from the crash without a scratch? Sometimes it is only later, when calm is restored, that the survivors of any tragedy are able to recognize the presence of Angels along their path. Does Angel Power make a difference?

Marissa believes she owes her life and her happiness to the Queen of Angels, who filled her broken life with Angel Power. Mark, in his dream, watched a small Angel dressed in blue do battle with a huge, hideous demon. His vision and path were forever altered that fateful night as he embraced Angel Power.

Marissa and the Angels

Twenty-nine? She looks no older. Terrible human misfortune overtook Marissa when she was seventeen years old. Angel Power restored beauty and peace to her life. It took Marissa painful years before she was able to access Angel Power. Her story contains many tools that are offered to spare others the years it took Marissa to access the power of Angels. Her lessons are insights for those who seek Angel Power in the midst of great sorrow.

Marissa was raised in a small town in Spain where the people never even thought of locking the doors of their tiny Mediterranean houses. When she was seventeen years old, innocent and quite naïve, her family moved to New York. Unsuspecting, Marissa went to school to learn English. No one had told her about the problems of life in a big city. One day as she sat on a bench waiting for the doors of the school to open, a man dragged her into the nearby park. He stabbed her eight times and raped her. Two mysterious "kind ladies" rescued her.

Let us hear Marissa's story in her own words:

> It was springtime, about six-thirty in the evening, I was stabbed eight times and raped. I was in intensive care for more than a week. Because the authorities thought my assailant was the Son of Sam, I had to be guarded by police at all times. It was considered dangerous for any of his victims to stay in a public hospital, so the authorities sent me home with round-the-clock

security. I had to be brought back to the hospital every morning. My right hand was paralyzed because the assailant beat it so badly and cut the muscle that goes down my arm. I had to have daily physical therapy to try to restore movement. My eyes were so severely injured that I could not see.

During the attack he kept hitting my eyes with the back of his knife. Every time I would get up, he stabbed me; then either he kicked me with his feet or threw me against a rock and hit my head. After a while he became quiet. I thought he had left. I tried again to get up. He would stab me again. This happened seven times. Each time he beat me more violently. He said, "I'm going to kill you like all the others." He constantly talked during the attacks. The last time he hit me, the blow was so violent that I couldn't breathe.

When I realized that he was going to kill me, I began to pray. I said, "O God, at least let me see my mother so that I can explain to her what has happened to me." Then I said an Act of Contrition for all my sins to be ready to die. Suddenly I found myself praying to Saint Jude because he is the Saint of the Impossible. As I was falling, I cried, "Saint Jude please let me see my mother alive!" I saw the image of Saint Jude interiorly before I collapsed.

When the assailant thought I was almost dead, he stabbed me for the eighth time and raped me. He kept talking the whole time.

I kept praying. Then I was unconscious for a while. When I awakened, I was afraid to get up. I kept fading in and out of consciousness. It was dark and it was cold. I tried to crawl. I tried to get up again and I passed out. When I awoke, I was extremely thirsty and bitterly cold.

I realized I had to get help, or I would bleed to death. I could hear the cars from the expressway. I could see the brightness of the lights of the cars, but I could not see. I crawled along the ground by touch so that I could discover where the street was. Then I got up. At the time, I thought my choice was to throw myself in front of a car and be run over or to stay in the park and be beaten and raped some more.

I prayed, "I'm sorry God, but I have to get this terrible nightmare over with." Then I threw myself in front of an oncoming car. I could hear the air from the brakes as the car stopped. I heard a lady get out of the car. She started screaming, "Oh, my God, there is a girl with blood all over her! I almost hit her with the car. I think she is dead!"

Then I heard another person come toward me. A kind and gentle lady with a very soothing voice covered me with a blanket. She was very loving to me. I was so thirsty that all I could think of was water. I begged her for a drink. A man's voice said, "If she has internal hemorrhaging, water will kill her. Don't give her water." The kind lady spoke gently and reassuringly to me. She calmed my hideous fear. I think I would have died of fright if she had not helped me.

When the ambulance arrived, the doctor immediately asked, "Did she have water?" The kind lady said they had not given me anything to drink. The doctor said, "She has strong internal hemorrhaging." The kind lady said, "I know, but she will be well."

In the ambulance I asked the doctor to take the knife out of me because it hurt me so much. He told me there was no knife in me. But I could feel the knife. He said that I was feeling the stab wounds, but there was no knife in me. He was very kind to me and held me in his arms because I was so afraid and had so much pain from the knife wounds.

When we arrived at the hospital, there were policemen everywhere around me. They told me that they were going to have to perform surgery without anesthesia because I had lost so much blood. They fastened my arms to the side of a bed and the doctor leaned close to me. He said, "I need to perform an incision without anesthesia. It's going to hurt a little bit." I was suffering terribly from thirst.

Four incisions were made to insert four tubes into my lungs. As the fourth tube was inserted, I felt a terrible heat in my head and heard a boom sound. Then I went through a tunnel and at the end of the tunnel I felt very much at peace.

It was a peace that I had never known before. Then I saw scenes of my childhood. It was not like a picture. I was actually living those scenes. I was with my great-grandmother, whom I loved so very much. I saw my mom ironing. I heard the phone ring. Then I saw my body lying below me on a table. It was like a used vehicle. I didn't care about it at all. I was glad to be out of it. It was nothing. I had no attachment to it. I just saw a body lying there in a pool of blood. Then I saw a doctor who came in and said, "We have lost her." Another doctor said, "Let's go for it!"

The medical team hooked things to the body and I saw my body jump, almost like jump-starting a car. Suddenly I was back in my body, and the pain was close to unbearable. One of the doctors said, "We need to find her mother. We are probably going to need to remove a lung. We need signed authorization for that. If she dies, at least we have done everything we can for her."

When my mother came in, she said, "I don't recognize this girl. She is all beaten and covered with blood." I couldn't talk because of the tubes. My heart was already broken, but when Mom didn't even know me, I just felt despair. Then Mom asked what I had been wearing when I came to the hospital. When the nurse showed her the knitted sweater she had made for me for Christmas, Mom fell down on the floor clutching the bloody sweater. "My baby! My baby! Oh God, what have they done to my baby?" she was crying. I just wanted to hold on to my mom, but they wouldn't let her touch me. Then they took her away.

Later when they let my mom into intensive care to see me, she fainted. My face was so injured that people could not stand to look at me. The nurses cried. Even some of the doctors cried. I had to stay without anesthesia or water for forty-eight hours to see if my condition would stabilize. The worst pain was the thirst.

Since the doctors didn't know if my assailant had any type of venereal disease, they kept pouring a red liquid antiseptic all over me and into the open wounds. It burned so badly that I could hardly stand the pain. With the tubes in my lungs, every breath and every movement was sheer torture. After forty-eight hours I received an injection and went into a deep sleep. Thanks to God I did not lose my eyesight. My arm is still not healed after twelve years, but I have some motion.

A woman police officer had to guard me all the time. The attacker was at large, and the police knew his pattern. He would stalk his victim. He knew I was alive because the newspapers carried the story of the attack. The other women he killed were all similar to me—long dark hair.

I had to go to the trial of the person the police said had attacked me. First I had to go to a lineup of suspects. It was not easy to recognize my assailant because the other attorneys disguised him completely. They made him wear long hair and a hat. When he attacked me, he was wearing a Mohawk haircut with reflecting sunglasses. I looked through the window at the lineup. There he was! He had a gang type of walk. He came toward me. When he got near me, though the authorities told me he could not see me, he began twitching his eye—a type of blink that he did constantly while he was attacking me.

Right away I recognized him. I said, "I think that's him!" His attorney said that it was an invalid identification because I only said "I think. . . ." So my attorney asked if the man would speak—he had spoken and made sounds the whole time the attack was occurring. They would not let him speak. So he went back in the line and I looked at each of the men in the lineup very carefully. I recognized the hands of the attacker. I had no doubt and said, "That's him!"

I had to testify at the trial. It turned out that he had done this same thing to other women. The only other one who was still alive was a medical doctor. She came to the trial, but when she saw him, she just kind of screamed silently and kept gasping for air. The medics had to take her out of the courtroom.

He admitted that all the other women died. It came out at the trial that he belonged to a satanic cult. He testified that I fought him back worse than any other woman he had ever attacked. He said he thought he had killed me.

My life was horrible after that. I would go from church to church and question Jesus. "How could You let that happen to me? What have I ever done to deserve such brutal cruelty? I lived in a small town; I never did anything bad. I always tried to be good. Why me?" I was very bitter. I prayed to Jesus and I constantly asked Him many times why He let this terrible attack happen to me. I was very angry. I knew I did not deserve this horror. I kept questioning Jesus. I could not forgive.

I did not let anybody get close to me. I never talked about my experience. If you met me, you would not have known that I was raped or stabbed. It took me many years to even smile.

If it was not for the Blessed Mother and the healing she brought to me, my boys and I would still be living in fear, poverty, and bitterness. The most amazing thing is that after I forgave him, every day when I receive the Holy Eucharist, he is the number one on my list. I pray for his conversion first and then all the others in my life. I cannot explain it, but every day I feel he is getting closer to God, wherever he is. I don't question anymore "Why me?" There are so many people who go through worse things than I. Now I feel very much at peace.

Before, if I was in a room and someone would even mention rape, I would get up and leave. During those twelve years

I did not go to a psychologist or a psychiatrist. That process would have been more torture. It was really prayer and the help of the Blessed Mother with the little Rosary miracle she gave me that healed my life. Now I experience joy, peace, and love. If it wasn't for the Blessed Mother and the way she spoke to me—she spoke to me the way a mother speaks to a child, but with so much love. She was like . . . tiptoeing into the subject with me. It took someone with the special nature the Blessed Mother has to get me to speak about it.

I felt like the loneliest person on earth. Nothing made sense. I was in and out of deep depression. I was afraid. I was looking for someone to care for me. I got married for all the wrong reasons.

Through the years I started traveling a lot because of the job that I had. I was in Seattle, Washington, and I could not get a taxi. A kind lady stopped her car and offered me a ride to the hotel. She asked me, "Do you pray to the Blessed Mother?" I said no. She said, "You should. Then you will be much happier. You will never be without if you pray to the Blessed Mother." She gave me a little blue booklet, the Pietà Prayer Book. I took it home with me and started praying the prayers every day.

Then I started wanting to go to daily Mass. I would stay after Mass and pray all the prayers in the Pietà Prayer Book. I noticed that there was a small prayer group gathered after the Mass. They did not invite me to pray with them. I prayed, "Blessed Mother, those ladies are bothering me. They are praying the Rosary and I want to pray these prayers from the Pietà Prayer Book." This went on for three days. Then I asked the Blessed Mother, "If you want me to pray the Rosary first, I will do it." This particular prayer group said not only the Rosary but afterward they said the Seven Sorrows of the Blessed Mother Rosary. I began to pray with them every day.

My friend from Mexico told me that every time you pray the Seven Sorrows Rosary, you pray one for each of the wounds of Jesus Christ. Since I, too, had been stabbed seven times plus one, I started asking, little by little, with the help of Jesus, if He and the Blessed Mother wanted me to forgive.

My friends in the prayer group told me that the Blessed Mother is appearing in Medjugorje. They gave me some of her messages. One in particular really spoke to me in a special way. She said:

Dear children, if you want to be very happy, pray.
Pray always.
Live a simple, humble life.
Do not focus on the problems of the day.

*If you focus on the problems, you actualize them. God
wants you to accept divine peace,
live divine peace, and spread divine peace.*

I was not happy. I always felt bitter about the stabs and the rape.
I could not afford to go to Medjugorje. I never thought about
forgiving before. The Blessed Mother is telling us at Medjugorje that the way to peace is forgiveness. That's why I started
to ask Jesus and the Blessed Mother for the help to try to forgive. I even stopped asking Jesus, "Why did you let it happen
to me?" I found myself really asking them to help me forgive
my assailant. The visionaries said the Blessed Mother always
says pray, pray, pray and your questions will be answered. I made
a commitment to pray. I gave the Blessed Mother everything,
my life, my thoughts, my problems, everything. I was so committed to prayer that though I worked sixteen hours a day, I
got up every day at five to pray.

I began to desire to give my heart to Jesus and the Blessed
Mother. I wanted to leave my heart with them so that they
would work through me to forgive this person. Little by little I
began to forgive the rapist for up to seven of the stabbings.
There were seven stabs to the upper part of my body. The
eighth was done to the lower part of my body. That one I

could not face or forgive. I had eight sorrows [wounds]. The little Rosary only has seven sorrows.

A friend of mine who went to Medjugorje told me that if you send a letter to the Blessed Mother, she will answer you. So I got up at four o'clock in the morning and started to write a letter to the Blessed Mother. It looked more like a Bible than a letter! I put it in a red envelope. My friend didn't want to take the letter. I told her, "Not only are you going to take it, you are going to give it to Vicka" (one of the six visionaries). She took my letter to Medjugorje and gave it to (visionary) Ivan. He promised to give it to Vicka. When I heard that, I knew that the Blessed Mother would answer me. The same day my friend gave me Rosaries from Medjugorje for my sons and me.

Each night we started praying the Rosary at home. The more I prayed, the more I wanted to pray. I began getting up at five to pray the Pietà Prayer Book prayers that contain the Chaplet of the Holy Angels and the Seven Sorrows Rosary. Then I prayed the Joyful Mysteries of the Rosary. One day when I started praying the Seven Sorrows Rosary, on the seventh one I felt that the Blessed Mother spoke to me. It was an interior voice—very clear, very sweet. I heard her say,

My daughter,
I desire you to forgive that person
for the eighth wound that he inflicted upon you.

I was kneeling on the floor. I got up and sat down on the sofa. "Did I really hear a voice?" I asked myself. Then I heard the same voice say the same thing!

My daughter,
I desire you to forgive that person
for the eighth wound that he inflicted upon you.

When I heard her sweet voice again, I was immediately taken to the eighth wound. I could never face it after it happened. I never told anyone about it. Even when the doctor took my stitches out for the upper part, my mother was not allowed to stay for the eighth one. He said, "Please tell your mother to leave the room." She didn't know. I told her that the doctor just wanted to talk to me. It was so horrible that I couldn't say anything. The nurses who were helping the doctor take the stitches out of the eighth wound were crying. One said, "What demon did this to you?" The other said, "Even animals aren't this vicious!" I buried my feelings and memories. I planned never to talk or think about it again.

Now the Blessed Mother was asking me to forgive the eighth wound. I was very upset that somebody would know what happened to me. I stood up. I was deeply shaken and I retorted, "How do you know my secret?" The Blessed Mother's voice was so sweet that I was totally surprised when she said,

My child, I know everything that happened to you.

I said, "Blessed Mother, I can't forgive him, but if you want him to be forgiven, ask Jesus Christ. Anything you ask, He gives you. He forgives everybody. But I can't forgive. I can't even face it." My son interrupted me, and I quickly left my prayer thoughts and got busy in the house. We got dressed, packed lunches, got into the car, and prayed the Rosary on the way to school.

After I dropped the children off at school, I went to Mass. After Mass I stayed to pray the Rosary with the prayer group. Then we prayed the little Rosary of the Seven Sorrows of the Blessed Mother. As we reached the seventh sorrow, I looked at the statue of the Blessed Mother. In my heart I again heard her ask me again to forgive that eighth wound. I said, "I'm sorry, Blessed Mother, I just can't, but if this is really coming from you, I want to touch the shoulder of the lady in front of me and whatever comes out of her mouth I will accept as you speaking to me." I put my hand on the shoulder of the lady in front of me. She turned around and said, "The Blessed Mother is talking to you. Please listen to her."

I prayed, "But Blessed Mother, this Seven Sorrows Rosary only has seven sorrows. I have eight. I need one more proof that it is really you talking to me—that it is really you who wants me to forgive." As we were finishing the seven sorrows, suddenly I felt my Rosary growing in my hand! I couldn't believe what I was feeling and I was afraid to look! I sat down and the words just tumbled out of my mouth: "Something very strange is happening. I think the Blessed Mother is asking me to forgive the eighth wound! I think my Rosary has eight wounds!" Nobody understood what I was saying, but they took the Medjugorje Rosary from my hands and everyone counted the beads. It had eight sets of beads, not seven! I fell on my knees right away and I said, "I'm sorry, Blessed Mother. I didn't know it mattered to you so much. For you I forgive him the eighth wound."

I fixed my eyes upon the life-size statue of Mary in the church. At that moment in my heart I heard the voice of the Blessed Mother:

My beloved daughter,
you must forgive him with your heart for the eighth
wound.

Suddenly the Blessed Mother was beside me with her arms around me. I recognized the same kindness and protection that I felt that dreadful night in the park when the kind lady covered me with a blanket and soothed my terror.

I felt the nearness of the Blessed Mother all around me. She spoke to me so close that I heard her sweet voice in my heart:

> **My precious**
> **daughter,**
> **you are able to forgive.**

I totally forgave at that moment. I told everyone about the eighth wound. I said I forgave from my heart. I apologized for asking the Blessed Mother for so many proofs that it was coming from her. Just then there was a powerful scent of roses that filled the church. We all began to pray and thank God, and thank the Blessed Mother and all the angels. Everyone was crying, hugging each other. We experienced a tremendous unity. We experienced a glow . . . like time had stopped. We were in front of the Blessed Sacrament. It was powerful. All the graces began to pour upon me. I felt as if an enormous weight had been lifted. I was finally free.

(Later, by interior illumination in prayer, the Blessed Mother told me that by forgiving from the heart I was healed. For a brief second, I saw the Judgment. The Blessed Mother most gently explained that when my turn arrives to come before Jesus, as all people do, if I hold offenses against me which I have refused to forgive, Jesus will be unable to forgive me. I have done things that need forgiveness. By forgiving my assailant, I was cleansed also. I was releasing him from some kind of bondage that also freed me.)

Marissa's friends say a strange thing happened after that. The pain and the years began to roll off her. She began to radiate a certain joy, a lightness of heart that was unmistakable. She and her little sons are happy.

Why was Marissa's life saved? She prayed to God and to Saint Jude, the patron of hopeless cases, as she faced certain death. Marissa asked that she might see her mother. The Blessed Mother of Jesus, who has been called the Queen of the Angels from the beginning of Christendom, was sent to her.

Marissa learned that the fire of love consumes nonlove. The eternal love of the Blessed Mother of Jesus filled her gaping wounds of bitterness. Her presence allowed Marissa to experience that God is Love. Marissa learned that those who do not trust God suffer endlessly. As Marissa made the commitment and began to pray fervently, she realized that God's love makes all things well.

One month before her annulment was final, Joseph came to her house to do some work. He was everything Marissa had prayed for. They were married a year later. Joseph even shares a birthday with the Blessed Mother, September 8th. Marissa is a beautiful, radiant, joy-filled young woman, laughing and smiling and filled with peace. She is a pleasure to be around. She is happy. She has Angel Power. God's ways never fail.

SONG OF THE QUEEN OF ANGELS

Forgiveness comes from God through His Love.

Forgiveness is the sweet balm of His Love.

It is in forgiveness that God's children are free to love.

Forgiveness is the key to love.

Forgiveness is a sublime affirmation of God's Power to make all things well.

Forgiveness of all wrongs is trust in God's Providence.

Forgiveness is the human response to God's Governance of the Cosmos.

Angelic Warnings and Invitations in Dreams

Throughout history God has manifested His Will to people through dreams. Angels are involved in our dreams. Dreams are part of the mystery of human suffering as well as part of enlightenment. Few people understand dreams.

The birth, life, death, resurrection, and ongoing presence of Jesus Christ in the world was and still is announced by Angels in person and in dreams and celestial signs. The suffering of Joseph of the Coat of Many Colors fed nations as he was being prepared to lead the faithful through an arduous famine. The Old Testament chronicles how Joseph counseled the Pharaoh and rose to the heights of power in Egypt because he had an exquisite gift for interpreting dreams.

All people on earth do suffer at some time. Some suffer more than others. Suffering somehow prepares us for our places in Paradise. It is the "sandpaper" that redefines and refines the beauty of each person. Suffering is paradoxically a great gift. It serves as a beacon of Truth. Suffering is permitted by God. How we accept suffering is our gift to Him. All religions understand this. It is through faith in God's Word, His Covenant, that His children are able to accept the suffering He allows. All suffering is for someone. God knows why He gives the suffering and when He will take it away. It is through trust in His Providence that His children bear their suffering in peace.

Those who access Angel Power bear suffering surrounded with God's Angels of consolation. Few if any escape suffering. With Angel Power, suffering, though painful, becomes a path of light. That path of light leads to incredible joy.

Those who experience no peace in suffering can quickly recognize that they are in great need of making some decisions. The first question to be answered is: Am I able to do anything to alleviate or eliminate this suffering that brings me no peace? If so, will my response (to the suffering) harm anyone else? When the suffering can be alleviated or eliminated without harming anyone else, then a person is duty bound to seek a remedy. God does not ask us to suffer needlessly simply for the sake of suffering.

When suffering cannot be eliminated or alleviated, a person has no choice but to endure. For those who access Angel Power, even the most difficult moments are somehow humanly tolerable. The Christians who were fed to the lions in the early days of the Church astounded the jeering mobs, for they radiated joy and peace and love. Extraordinary conversions flowed from their serenity in suffering. "Who is this unseen God who fills their hearts with such joy?" the people began to wonder. The martyrs of the Roman Circus were totally abandoned to God's Providential Care and live on in the hearts of the faithful even now. They experienced Angel Power, for Angels are spirits of pure peace.

Many people all over the world have dreams that warn and prepare them for events and circumstances that are difficult to understand or tolerate. Other dreams are simply nightmares. Who knows where the human spirit roams when we are asleep? Jesus released His Spirit into the hands of His Father when He cried out from the cross:

Father, into Thy Hands I commend My Spirit.

People who follow that example and commend their spirit into the hands of God before sleep may find solutions to difficult and often incomprehensible dreams as He sends Angel Power to guard and guide them in their dreams.

Mark's Story

Mark was in seventh grade. He lived in a modest house with his parents, grandparents, four brothers, and three sisters in an Italian-families neighborhood interspersed with Polish and Mexican. Neither of Mark's parents finished high school. His father belonged to the meat packers' union. Mark was an altar server and sang in the church choir, though his family had long ago stopped attending church.

One night Mark had a dream that changed his life. He saw his entire neighborhood in black and white. It was totally fenced off—inaccessible. Everything was lifeless. Where Mark stood, however, everything was in Technicolor: everything was vibrant and bursting with life.

Mark, filled with boyish curiosity, knew he had to climb the fence and find out why everything on the other side of the fence was dead. Though his family's house looked haunted and was covered with dead vines, dead leaves, dead branches from dead trees, Mark bolted into the scene and entered his home. The interior was misty. There were cobwebs everywhere. The smell was putrid, as if everything was rotten.

Mark saw a huge, faceless, black-shrouded figure clothed in filth. It hovered even nearer to him. Terrifying, hideous laughter, a din of horror, spewed from the shrouded demon. The eerie, ridiculing laughter rocked the haunted house—the walls, the ceiling, the filthy windows. It was crackling laughter, loud, deep, ugly, mocking.

Mark lunged at the black shroud: "You're the source of all this death, aren't you?" But Mark's fists hit heavy mist. The obnoxious laughter now taunted him. Mark pointed at the creature he saw, but he could not touch it to push it away. He started to pray, "Our Father Who art in Heaven, Hallowed be Thy Name."

The shrouded creature shrieked as if in mortal pain. Mark felt an immense power coming from the prayer surge through him as he continued to point at the grotesque creature of unbridled hate: "Thy Kingdom come, **Thy Will** be done on earth as it is in Heaven."

Mark realized that his arm had become like a sword of piercing light empowered by the words of the prayer he recited. In amazement Mark momentarily stopped praying. Suddenly the huge creature grew in intensity and lunged at Mark in a rage of cruelty fired with pernicious laughter. Instantly Mark cried out, "God, our Father, give us this day our daily bread!"

The creature stopped in midair as the prayer reactivated the light from Mark's pointed finger. It became a scorching laser sword causing the shrouded creature to dematerialize. Primordial fear gripped Mark. He could hear the grisly abomination of the mocking laughter, but he couldn't see the demon!

Mark, sweating profusely now and quaking with perilous fear, screamed, "God, our Father, forgive us our trespasses as we forgive those who trespass against us!"

Mark suddenly saw a little angel, dressed in blue, in the corner of the room. It was pointing into the air. Mark cried out,

Father deliver us from evil!
Father deliver us from evil!
Father deliver us from evil!

as he pointed his arm in the direction shown him by the little blue angel. The prayer became so intense that Mark suddenly found himself in the midst of a tremendous explosion.

He realized that he was speeding through a tunnel. As Mark exited the tunnel, he saw himself standing in clouds up to his knees. He looked up and saw people all around him. They looked more real and alive than the people of Earth. He experienced a beauty and magnificence that were beyond his deepest longings.

Mark made eye contact with the people. He instantly was enveloped in the sweetness of pure love. He knew he was accepted, that he belonged, that he was totally loved. The people were wearing beautiful robes of glorious profusions of colors that were made of pure light, far more varied and brilliant than the mere colors of the rainbow.

Mark, though he had never met any of the people, knew each of them intimately with pure love. He recognized that he belonged to them and they belonged to him. He contained a fathomless profundity of love for each of them, more intense, more penetrating than his capacity to comprehend or feel. For a shining moment Mark simply surrendered to the mystery of real love. At that moment he saw Jesus in the center of all the people.

Jesus looked even more splendorous than all the other glorious people who were gathered there. Mark's eyes met Jesus' eyes. They were locked. Mark saw Truth. Mark met Love. Mark encountered eternity in Jesus' Divine Eyes. Mark was complete.

Jesus raised His right hand. The motion dislodged the eye contact. He held a scarlet ribbon with a heart at the end. Jesus placed the heart into Mark's chest and Mark felt a deep, burning sensation.

The burning pain was so intense that Mark suddenly found himself sitting up in his bed. The searing pain continued for about thirty minutes. A part of Mark was dying. The foolish desires and self-centered longings of the seventh-grader melted into the cauldron of illusion as Angel Power opened Mark's eyes to the light of Truth. He arose from his bed and walked to the window. The morning was breaking through the darkness of yesterday.

"Jesus is alive! He knows me! I will be with Him again! Nothing else is important!" Mark said quietly to the Angels he knew surrounded him.

"I shall serve God with my life just as you do!" Mark said to the Angels, though he didn't see them. It was enough that he knew. The room was filled with light. The words of Saint Matthew became emblazoned into Mark's spirit that morning:

> When the Son of Man comes in his glory, and all the angels with him, He will sit upon his glorious throne, and all the nations will be assembled before him. And he will separate them one from another, as a shepherd separates the sheep from the goats. He will place the sheep on his right and the goats on his left. Then the king will say to those on his right, "Come, you who are blessed by my Father. Inherit the kingdom prepared for you from the foundation of the world. For I was hungry and you gave me food, I was thirsty and you gave me drink, a stranger and you welcomed me, naked and you clothed me, ill and you cared for me, In prison and you visited me.

Then the righteous will answer him and say: "Lord, when did we see you hungry and feed you, or thirsty and give you a drink? When did we see you a stranger and welcome you, or naked and clothe you? When did we see you ill or in prison, and visit you?

And the king will say to them in reply, "Amen, I say to you, whatever you did for one of these least brothers of mine, you did for me."

Then he will say to those on his left, "Depart from me, you accursed, into the eternal fire prepared for the devil and his angels. For I was hungry and you gave me no food, I was thirsty and you gave me no drink, a stranger and you gave me no welcome, naked and you gave me no clothing, ill and in prison, and you did not care for me.

Then they will answer and say, "Lord, when did we see You hungry or thirsty or a stranger or naked or ill or in prison, and not minister to your needs?"

He will answer them, "Amen, I say to you, what you did not do for one of these least ones, you did not do for me."

And these will go off to eternal punishment, but the righteous
to eternal life.—Matthew 25:31–46

Mark's life was dramatically altered after his mysterious and powerful
dream. The burning love he encountered in his dream remained in his heart,
propelling him to a career as president of an international nonprofit organiza-
tion that cares for the needs of people all over the world. Mark and his staff labor as "workers in the vineyard," aspiring to be Angels of God's Mercy who
help others each day. Mark knows that only those who have been and are
loved are capable of loving others. Love begets love. Angel Power is the story
of Love.

Meditation

Beware, My children.
The gift of conscience is a sharp sword.
When you sense pain in your conscience,
accept the pain as My Great Gift.
That pain pulls you back on the path to My Kingdom.

Those who experience no pain
when they disobey My Commandments
do not benefit from the gift of My Sword of Justice.
Love for Me. Trust My Ways.
I am the Way and the Truth and the Light for your journey
on the earth.
I am Life. All else is death.
Those who live in My Love never die.

Prayer

IN HONOR OF SAINT MICHAEL THE ARCHANGEL FOR

PROTECTION FROM ENEMIES

Almighty God, our Father, Creator and Ruler,
How kind is your Heart.
How generous and merciful are your ways.
Forgive us our mistakes O holy and patient Father.

Gentle, Divine Father, filled with love,
Allow Your Prince of the Heavenly Host,
Saint Michael the Archangel, trusted confidante of Your will,
To abide with us at every moment.

Loving, Divine Father, heal the consequences of our poor
    choices.
Send the Prince of your holy angels to defend, protect and
Remedy the circumstances that create enemies for us.
Bless our enemies. Graciously give them what they need.

Eternal Father, please grant Saint Michael the Archangel
The power to turn our enemies into loving, trusted colleagues.
May he present our lives to your fathomless mercy dear Father
In the name of our Lord and Savior, Jesus Christ, now and
forever. Amen.

Chapter Fourteen

Living with
Angel Power

❊❈❊

But as it is written: What eye has not seen,
and ear has not heard,
and what has not entered the human heart,
what God has prepared for those who love him.

—1 CORINTHIANS 2:9

The ways of God provide a clear path out of bondage for all those who have the courage and discipline to respond to God's Providential Love. Everyone's gifts are important to everyone else. Sometimes we are our own worst enemy. Without a clear vision of who we are, our inestimable worth in God's Plan, and the capacity to access the unfathomable power of God's Love in times of doubt and confusion, life can be a cauldron of aimless uncertainty. Precious gifts and talents that are unique and important to the well-being of everyone can lie fallow within us in the dysfunction of ignorance and be lost to the entire world forever.

Maggie's Story

Maggie had big blue eyes and lots of freckles. Though it was highly unusual in the small mill town for families to move in mid-year, Maggie showed up at eighth grade in November. She laughed quickly, and no one suspected that the home life of the eighth-grader was anything less than blissful.

Maggie quickly found a best friend in Mary Lou. Withdrawn and disciplined, Mary Lou was easily the best student in the class of fifty-eight children. She was different from the others. Her clothes were fine, and her mother came in a big car when the snow fell. Laughing, Maggie got a ride home, too, in the big car. The place where Maggie lived was modest. Not to worry, sang Mary Lou's mother. "Come home anytime with Mary Lou."

And Maggie did. Mary Lou was overjoyed to have a friend. They talked and played and dreamed of angels and fairy godmothers and of course Prince Charming, as young girls often do. When Christmas vacation came, Maggie spent every day at Mary Lou's house. There was so much work to do! The family was large. Everyone had chores. The work was fun for Maggie because there were so many people doing so much.

One day Maggie was assigned to scrub the kitchen floor with Mary Lou's youngest brother. The snow swirled in dancing patterns against every window of the massive four-story Connecticut stone house. Mary Lou's brother was cute. A chubby seven-year-old, he dreamed of football heroes and the airplanes he hoped to fly when he grew up. "We have to make this floor perfect!" he earnestly reassured Maggie as she dipped her hands into the bucket of scalding water for the first time. Did anyone scrub floors at her house? Maggie couldn't remember.

Maggie was happy. The big kitchen floor was finally finished. Now onto some Ping-Pong in the large recreation room on the lower level of the big house. Mary Lou's mother came in to inspect the kitchen floor. "What good children you are!" she said in praise. "But how sad your Guardian Angels must be. Look! You didn't scrub the area under the table."

"Oh no, Mummy!" exclaimed the exuberant seven-year-old. "My Guardian Angel knows we only forgot! Let's go, Maggie. The angels are watching. My Guardian Angel knows I always do everything right! I'm his best friend, and he can count on me." Maggie had never heard anything like this, but she soon learned that all the children in the family actually believed that there were thousands of angels who lived in the big house with them. They believed that the angels watched everything that they were doing and heard everything they were saying. The children laughed with genuine mirth at the foibles of their human duties and limitations. Being able to say "Good thing the angels know long division!" made difficult homework assignments palatable, and scrubbing kitchen floors became a heavenly project for the Angels who were watching.

When the time for eighth-grade graduation arrived, Mary Lou's mother found a beautiful dress for Maggie to wear at the local department store. "The angels just insisted that you would be glorious in this shade of pink!" she told the astounded Maggie.

Mary Lou received a scholarship to a fine boarding school in a distant city the next year. Maggie missed Mary Lou, but she had learned much. Her path out of the generational bondage of alcoholic parents was lighted by the patterns and habits that she began to learn in Mary Lou's home.

During ninth grade, when Maggie's dysfunctional parents were again faced with the prospect of moving to yet another location, Maggie was "found" by a neurosurgeon's wife, a friend of Mary Lou's mother. Maggie went to live with the neurosurgeon's family to help care for their four small children after school and on weekends.

After high school Maggie went to the local branch of the state university. At graduation Maggie giggled as she accepted her *summa cum laude* diploma, for she knew she looked glorious in the pink dress that was hidden by her black robe. The years spent with the neurosurgeon's family had reinforced for Maggie the attitudes and habits that bring personal success.

Maggie went to medical school and became a pediatrician. The glorious joy in Maggie's heart is like a spark that ignites laughter and mirth. Maggie married a Hindu doctor, who treasures her relationship with angels.

Kindness is her style, they say of Maggie at the hospital where she works. Maggie does not know anxiety. In her mind she discourses continuously with the invisible angels, who enfold her in a phalanx of protection. They carry her prayers, petitions, and constant thanksgiving up through all the entire Nine Choirs and into the Heart of God.

Maggie is quietly referred to as a healer at the hospital, though her mirthful laughter would ring like a carillon if anybody suggested such a thing in her presence. When she did her rotation in the intensive care unit, one young intern said of Maggie, "Peace is her name. Peace is her game."

Maggie's husband says of her, "Maggie speaks only Truth. She thinks only of those things that are lovely and pure. She is honorable, she is just, she is gracious. She loves the angels. She is like the angels!"

Angel Power and Attitude and Habits

The first tool that is needed to access the power of angels is a clear vision of where you are going. Once your destination is chosen, set the compass of your life. Keep the rudder of your boat (your moment-by-moment choices) directed toward the shores of your destination. Let nothing take you off course once you have set the destination. Stay highly focused at all times.

Discipline yourself to observe everything on your path. God sends opportunities for enlightenment and human advancement to you on the wings of angels every day. What reactions do your day-to-day obligations and commitments bring forth from you? What do you need to change to be effective? What are you able to change? Illusion dies slowly, for seeing Truth requires vision and courage. With Angel Power comes vision and the courage to make correct choices.

Develop the capacity to listen to the rhythm of the cosmos. Scrupulous honesty is the watchdog of integrity. Integrity is the banner of Truth. The first person we need to be honest with is ourselves. If we take a good look at ourselves and learn that we do not like who or what we are, that we do not like the circumstances that seem to hold us hostage, the next step is to ask ourselves, "What am I able to change?"

All Are Flowers of God's Love

A young man was dying from complications of AIDS. He heard of a prayer community where a nun cares for AIDS patients. Some of those who are under her care are cured of the incurable disease. With no other avenue of hope, the young man asked his friends to take him to the prayer community.

Desperately ill, he was assigned by the nurse nun to a bed in a large, airy room filled with sunlight. She welcomed him with much warmth and told him in a voice everyone in the corridor could hear, "Everyone here is a gift! You all are my flowers of God's Love. It is not by coincidence that any of you has come here. Each of you has something to give and to receive. Believe in the immense value of one another, because we are a family, and we choose to live here to love and serve one another. Each job that is assigned to each of us is important, not only for you but for me and everyone else here too. The one who has no job has no life."

As the nun established the man in his room, she continued: "There is nothing but honesty here. We all receive the self-discipline it requires to be honest through the illness that affects us all. Illness cures illusion. Each of us here comes from a background where we understand compassion. Each of us bears the pain and joy of one another.

"Lies strangle the joy out of every life. The truth is that you and everyone else here is a beautiful gift to the world. You will not tolerate untruth in yourself, as you see how it hurts all of us. Your past does not condemn you. Your sickness is not a punishment. Truth is a beam of sunlight in the arctic cold of mistakes, misunderstandings, sickness, and pain.

"Today is a new day to bathe yourself in the warmth of God's love. You are becoming a well person. Sickness has no power over you, for the past has no power over you here. You have much work to do now.

"You are assigned the job of fasting from maximum comfort. Since your body is too weak just now to do more, I will arrange your pillow a small level below the maximum comfort zone for one minute each hour. In that way you may offer your small sacrifice of maximum comfort to God as a gift of gratitude for the value of your life. As you offer your sacrifice, high-ranking angels draw near to collect it and carry it to God. All of us here receive the blessings and light of the high-ranking angels as they draw near to you. During your one-minute fasts speak to the angels. Tell them for us that we thank them for your presence." Her eyes twinkled with a hint of the vast pools of knowledge she was sprinkling upon the very sick young man.

Over the next days and weeks the actual presence of the angels entered into the conscious awareness of the young man. His one-minute fasts from maximum comfort became two minutes. It was not long before he was able to sit up on his own in his bed. He began sharing the thoughts that came to him as he spoke to the angels with others, who also spoke of angels.

He didn't die. He went into a state of remission that doesn't usually occur in cases like his. He works in the fields every morning now and he tells people that angels work with him. His friends come to visit so that they, too, can listen to his tales of angels.

Angel Power and Spiritual Guides

Scrupulous honesty moves us from unconscious living to active participation in the currents of our own life. Sometimes we need mentors who know and live Truth. It takes courage to find a mentor and to pay the price that total honesty requires. Anyone who lives in Truth will help another person who sincerely desires to live in Truth, for Truth begets Truth, just as illusion begets illusion. Those who live in Truth know angels. They adopt the habits and patterns of angels. They become "angels" to others.

Maggie's story demonstrates the success she was able to make of her life because she had the vision to recognize patterns that succeed. She also had the courage to leave her family and work for others who could mentor her in the attitudes and habits that achieve healthy goals. The people who helped Maggie were angels of God's Mercy to her. They opened their hearts and homes to her, but they required her participation and cooperation. Maggie's work at the hospital demonstrates how she has integrated the lessons she learned into the care she gives the sickest patients there. The peace she bears in her demeanor is an outward sign of the tranquillity of her heart. Maggie knows angels well. She has Angel Power.

Angelic Channels of Love

God's Divine Power flows through angels, who are perfectly pure, transparent channels of His Love. It is necessary to discipline our minds and bodies toward purity so that we are better able to access the angels. Prayer, fasting, and meditation are stepping-stones to pure Truth. Those who pray, fast, and meditate develop discernment to recognize the opportunities that God places before each of His children constantly. Prayer and fasting protect people from illusion. A test for the authenticity of those who would be our mentors involves the level of peace and joy that we encounter in their presence. When there is no peace, there is no love. Where there is no love, God is not present.

Prayerful fasting is a speedy road to peace. We begin fasting by completely forgiving ourselves for all the wrongs we have done to others. To make such forgiveness effective, we must totally and completely forgive all the wrongs that have ever been done against us by anyone.

The next step is to ask the angels to bless all those we have ever harmed. God has enough power and might to heal and restore the worst mistakes of all humanity. All it takes is faith in His Presence and trust in His Love and Power.

Then we ask the angels of God to surround us and fill us with their love and protection.

The next step is to accept the rule of the cosmos that we must make restitution for the wrongs we have done to others. When a little child hits a softball through the neighbor's window, he will tell the neighbor that he is sorry. But he must also replace the broken window. Here is the joyous secret of work. As the child does chores for the neighbor to pay for the window, he lightens the load of the neighbor. He exchanges his youthful exuberance for the dollars it will cost to buy the pane of glass he broke. He shares the life of his neighbor, and his neighbor shares his life. In that way mistakes become mutual gifts of love.

It is not always possible to make amends so directly, particularly if much time has passed. We do what we reasonably can each day to help, encourage, share, and cheer up those on our path as a tool of restitution for the situations and circumstances that we were not able to remedy at the time.

Faith and trust in God draw down all the angels of Paradise to the world of human beings. Where angels dwell, love reigns.

Those who allow perceived harm or misfortune to become a permanent negative fixture in their memory make this injury real. It is easier to forgive any harm done to us when injury is seen against the wider horizon of God's Power to renew and restore us. Even the smallest of cuts on our hand will not heal if we constantly touch it, rub it, and continuously reopen the wound.

The balm of God's Love and our own forgiveness heal every wound. When all our hurts and misfortunes are entrusted to God's Mercy, angels have projects they dearly enjoy. Expect great things of angels! They are truly our best friends. Bless God's power. Forgive those who offend or injure. Trust God to make lemonade out of lemons. Place everything in God's Hands. Then peace the world cannot give settles in the place of the injury. Scars are stars in the divine economy of God's Will.

Precious Angels of God's Love

When Janëll was quite young, she received a magnificent doll, more beautiful, she was certain, than any doll that was ever created. The doll's hat was white with pink ribbons streaming down over the wide straw brim. Her lovely pink dress discreetly covered the toes of her white silk slippers. The doll's face seemed filled with joy and wonder at her own creation. Janëll's heart glowed with love and gratitude, for the doll was exquisitely beautiful. She named her Scarlett.

One day when Janëll came home from school, she found Scarlett on the floor. Her dress was in a heap. Her hat was missing and her arms, legs, and head had been dismembered from her body. "My poor precious Scarlett," Janëll cried. As the tears streamed down her cheeks, she lovingly kissed Scarlett's face and arms and legs and trunk. Janëll found a most beautiful hatbox. She tenderly placed the parts of Scarlett in tissue paper in the hat box with the promise that "the angels will fix you." The hatbox contained Janëll's secret treasure. Janëll kept it hidden and carried it with her to all her homes after she grew up.

When Janëll was forty years old, her children, ages fifteen, thirteen, and ten, planned a special birthday dinner for their mother. Before the cake was served, Janëll's oldest son said, "Surprise!" Triumphantly Janëll's ten-year-old carried Scarlett into the dining room.

She was magnificent once again! Scarlett was more beautiful than any doll that was ever created. Her hat was white with pink ribbons streaming down over the wide straw brim. Her lovely pink dress discreetly covered the toes of her white silk slippers. The doll's face seemed filled with joy and wonder at her own restoration.

Janëll's heart exploded with love and gratitude, for her children had secretly made Scarlett exquisitely beautiful again. Love closes all wounds. Love heals and restores. Janëll saw each of her children as precious angels of God's love as she kissed Scarlett's face and shed tears of joy. The children, too, kissed Scarlett and felt their mother's love.

For Beginners Only

It is not by coincidence that you have obtained this book. You are about to unlock the greatest secret in the history of humanity. You are a masterpiece of God's Love! He loves you unconditionally, just as you are, as you were, and as you will be. Angel Power is waiting for you.

Bob and Midge own their own business, but neither has ever owned a Bible. They do not know what the term *sacred texts* means. Bob and Midge just learned about their Guardian Angels. They do not know how to talk to their Guardian Angels. How do they begin?

There are many like Bob and Midge. The following suggestions are offered as a starting point in the journey to access Angel Power:

1. Take the Angel Insurance Policy on page xxi seriously. Study its provisions and make them part of your life.

2. Each morning as you awaken and every night before you fall asleep, reread the following:

MESSAGE FROM A GUARDIAN ANGEL

You are well, my beloved friend.
You are God's treasure.
Can't you see me now?
Ah, you still harbor some fear?
It covers lack of faith, lack of trust.
Pray for strong faith, for hope.
When these virtues
Join the love in your heart
you will be whole
When you are whole, you are holy.

3. During the day, from time to time, repeat the following words:

> *Guardian Angel of mine, do you know me?*
> *Guardian angel of mine, do you love me as I am?*
> *Guardian Angel of mine, help my unbelief (or whatever your need or*
> *problem may be).*

Prayer allows solitude to caress your soul and nourish and comfort it. Cherish your moments of prayer. They are divine gifts of God's Love.

4. After saying the prayer to your Guardian Angel, listen carefully for several seconds. With enough practice you will recognize your Guardian Angel's voice. Let nothing interrupt the moments of silent listening. (WARNING: Any inspirations that do not bring you peace, confidence in God's Ways, or help are *not* coming from your Guardian Angel. Quickly discard them by prayer.)

5. Rent an inspirational video and watch it. There are many from which to choose, such as *The Ten Commandments*, *The Life of Jesus*, *Quo Vadis*, *The Robe*, *The Song of Bernadette*, *Schindler's List*, *Gandhi*, *The Chosen*, *It's a Wonderful Life*. Think about the video and try to recognize its personal message to you.

6. Buy or borrow a Bible or a sacred text of your choice. Find a few minutes of quiet each day and read several lines of the Bible or other sacred text. Then think about the words you have read during the day.

7. Fast twice a week, or abstain from something you crave. Meditate on the effect such fasting produces on your appetite, your nervous system, your temper, your sense of self-worth. Then offer the discomfort associated with the fast on behalf of someone you love and want to help. You gain two blessings from such a gift: You strengthen your authority over your own body and its cravings and you spiritually reach out to help another.

8. Practice the following breathing exercise at the first moment of stress: Slowly inhale and experience the air as God's personal Love for you; as you exhale experience the air as your personal gratitude to God. Focus only on the mutuality of God's Love for you and your gratitude to God. Continue breathing consciously in this way until the stress departs. Frequently practice breathing in God's love and exhaling your gratitude. This breathing exercise allows you to receive and give love energy. It energizes with God's Divine Love.

9. After several weeks of this program, begin to include each day some of the tools that follow. If you persevere, you will soon enjoy a most glorious, permanently rewarding relationship with your own Guardian Angel and all the holy angels of the Nine Choirs.

Angel Power and Purity of Thought

A powerful tool that speedily accesses Angel Power is the mental determination to judge no one. Judgment belongs to God alone. Those who live a life of abundance and happiness do not enter into the quicksand of human judgment against another. The Lord said that vengeance is His alone.

Physical and mental discipline facilitate access to the angels. We choose what will dwell in our conscious mind. It is personal choice how we fill our mind. Happiness is always a personal choice. Ettie Hillison wrote some of the most beautiful, inspiring thoughts of the twentieth century from Auschwitz. Circumstances do not the person make. Human greatness is manifested in one's reaction to circumstances.

Free will is the most precious gift of God's Love that human beings possess. Do not squander that gift on things that pass away. Awaken each day to the glorious opportunities God gives only to you to know Him, treasure Him, and to experience His Fathomless Love for you. Angel Power helps us to recognize God in our lives and to respond to His Presence. That action is true freedom.

Angels are able to guard our mind, thoughts, and emotions by warning us when we accept images, ideas, or commitments that destroy our peace. Mental discipline leads to mental hygiene and is a trait we acquire as we learn to access Angel Power on the psychic level.

Before we act, it is vital to ask the following questions: "What are the ramifications? What impact does this decision have on me now? What results will it yield five years from now? Who else will be affected? What is my responsibility to those people?" When we analyze the results of our deeds and their impact on others, we are able to make choices based on a higher level of consciousness.

Every act of ours has an effect. Certain responses flow from every act. We are ultimately responsible for every thought, word, and deed of ours. Angel Power guides our ability to make informed choices based on Truth.

Because angels are beings of purity and perfection, they fulfill the law of cause and effect perfectly. We humans must bear the effects of what we have done and are doing to ourselves and to one another. Holding on to negative, unkind, and malevolent thoughts eradicates our ability to access Angel Power. Ungoverned emotional and physical appetites or outbursts upset the tranquillity and availability of Angel Power. Without Angel Power we slide into the world of illusion.

On our own power we cannot reach God. The chasm between the finite (that's us) and the infinite (God) is so vast that He alone can bridge the gap. And He does. The Word was made flesh and dwells among us in Jesus (John 1:14). God ministers to His Creatures through angels, through the Prophets (with the help of the angels), and through holy men and women (with the help of the angels). Angels are available to guard and guide our body, mind, and spirit. They bring the very power of God to our personal world. He has assigned them to us that we may attain union with God. Through Angel Power God returns His children to the Garden of Paradise.

Try to experience surprises every day. God is found in simple things. Think of His Angels. Their world is our world, but we do not enter into their world because we are so busy with events of the sensate world. Many people are exhausted looking for God in people and events. He comes to us in stillness. He hovers over us always. We are fish swimming in the sea of His Love. His Angels are ministers plenipotentiary of His Infinite, Unchanging Love. God is Love. Love begets love (John 17:23–26). He who loves resides in God and God in him. That is His Covenant with His People (John 17:23–26).

Angel Power and Tranquillity

Early-morning prayer of welcome to the holy angels sets the tone for a day of peace and harmony. The prayers included in this book are offerings of great love for the angels. Prayer helps us become aware of spiritual Truth. Prayer prevents spiritual atrophy. Prayer provides spiritual exercise so that we may grow in our capacity to access the spirit world. Prayer is armor against the constant attacks of the rebel spirits. Prayer unmasks illusion. Prayer draws Angel Power around us.

In order to hear the voice of God, we must discipline ourselves so that we preserve our mind, imagination, longings, and appetites in a state of tranquillity and peace.[1] Those who truly desire to live on a higher plane of awareness simplify their lifestyle. It takes courage to eliminate needless things from our life. It takes fortitude to eliminate worry. But after all, worry is really lack of trust in God's Ability to make all things well. Through prayer we learn to trust the Providence of God. Do not worry. Worry is lack of trust in God's Love for us.

Detachment that places all things, places, ideas, even dearly loved people in God's Heart of Love is true freedom. The purpose of detachment is to lead our soul into the depths of solitude. In that tranquillity and quiet we hear the voice of our Guardian Angel. Angel Power allows us to be attached to the spirit of Truth. Within that spirit is peace, joy, and abiding love.

Those who hear their Guardian Angels are trained to hear the voice of God. In order to hear the voice of God, we must also actively labor to become aware of and to overcome faults that attach themselves to our personality like leprous sores, draining life and abundance.[2] It is always God's Will that His children love and serve one another. Anything in our personality that revolts at loving or serving God, or another, deserves our careful scrutiny.

Prayer is a gentle way to become aware of our faults. Prayer accesses angels, who join us in carrying our requests to God. God kindly allows us to see Truth; in that light we are able to correct our faults with His Help. When we are shown our faults through failure, the cruelty of others, or any of the thousands of ways that they manifest, we often suffer much. It is far easier and more gentle to ferret out our faults ourselves through prayer, fasting, and the practice of virtue than to be overcome by them. Virtue begets virtue.

Human souls (that's us) are the receptors of the Divine Mysteries. The personal dispositions of our soul determine how much of the Divine Mysteries we receive.

Many people, out of ignorance, weakness, fear, or malevolence, access the negative power that flows from the rebel spirit corps.[3] They reap a life of relentless suffering, even though they are sometimes surrounded by material abundance. Those who have accessed negative power are often unaware that they possess counterfeit truth. Hints abound: broken relationships; destroyed careers; smug arrogance that poisons communities, families, churches, businesses, and governments. Negative energy flows from the darkness of nontruth. Negativity begets negativity. Darkness begets darkness.

The relentless suggestions of the rebel spirits lead to vice. The more deeply we become entrenched in vice, the more difficult it is to see clearly. Vice is like quicksand. Sometimes it is impossible to get out of the trap without the help of others. Angel Power is quite effective for those who desire to be released. Angels are extraordinary intercessors. When angels are included in human pursuits, victory means peace, joy, and love. Angels are truly our best friends, and the best friends of all those we love.

Individuals, families, groups, and nations can all fall into the quicksand of counterfeit truth. World Wars are one such example. Broken and destroyed families are yet another example. Cruelty, poverty, and suffering are the offspring of counterfeit truth.

For those who love God, all things work together for good. Goodness begets goodness.[4]

Angel Power and Tools of Recognition

A person warned is a person prepared. The deadly sins destroy Divine Light in us. Pride, envy, jealousy, anger, gluttony, lust, and sloth are the characteristics of the Evil One. Whom do we choose to emulate? Are we even aware of our own characteristics?

By prayer and fasting, God's children begin to acquire virtue. Angels help people to fast from those attitudes and temptations that lead to the deadly sins. God always asks His children to trust Him, to turn to Him that He might free them from the snarls that entangle their souls in deadly sins. God asks His children to pray more and to fast with great love, for fasting brings them the light to see Truth.

Demons have lurked in the hearts of humanity for centuries. Severe injuries create wounds that are festering grounds for the demons of nonforgiveness. These demons are passed on from generation to generation unless God's grace intervenes.

Our words are a barometer of the purity of our heart. By our words we announce to each person the condition of our heart. Demons of hate and lust and power and avarice pour into the world in both word and deed. Angels bear the light of Truth as they hover over God's children. As the evil spirits' traits are subjected to the light of Truth, God's children flee to His Arms for safety.

God our Father protects His children. Through His Son Jesus, God has freed all humanity from the demons that have lurked in human hearts and minds for centuries. There is no place in any heart for any presence but God's Love. As the tongue speaks, so the human heart is diagnosed. The father of lies loves darkness. He longs to dwell deep in God's children's Hearts.

God is Truth. The soul wounded by nontruth has no capacity to see God's Ways without prayer and fasting. All people can pray. All people can fast. God gives that light freely to those who ask. Through prayer and fasting, hearts sick with sin are purified. Satan and his lies are being unmasked all over the world in these times.

Angel Power and Tools of Discipline

There are many ways to find God. The following tools have proven to be highly effective for those who choose to live in communion with angels. They are offered as suggestions for those who want to access Angel Power.

1. Renounce heightened passions and inordinate desires

To accomplish this goal, personal discipline and discernment are necessary.

Excessive visual or audio entertainment that stimulates the imagination destroys the tranquillity that allows communication with the angels. What the eye sees and the ear hears must be carefully weighed against the horizon of our eternal goal.

Excessive eating and drinking create a sensual dullness that makes it difficult to hear the words of angels or to experience their presence. It is necessary to eat only what nourishes the body, but not necessarily what pleases the appetites.

2. Eliminate all anxiety

To accomplish this goal it is essential to meditate daily and to grow in virtue. The meditations that conclude this book are useful and should be read slowly and pondered for at least fifteen minutes each day.

A proper foundation for these meditations would include the reading of sacred texts early in the morning and before retiring for the night in order to ground the day in the word and ways of God. The sacred texts lead the human soul deep into the virtues of faith, hope, and charity. A soul who trusts God does not worry. A soul who loves God has no fear.

3. Love all your enemies

To accomplish this goal, ask your Guardian Angel to join you in fervent prayer for all those who have disturbed you, disappointed you, or created pain and harm for you. The Lord has said that vengeance belongs to Him alone. Ask your Guardian Angel to carry blessings to the Guardian Angels of your enemies. Ask your Guardian Angel to request the Guardian Angels of your enemies ways to protect you and spare you from any harm. Pray often the prayer for angelic protection from enemies on page 272.

Entrust your enemies to the mercy of God. Pray that God will bless your enemies and give them what they need. Choose not only to love these people but also to like them for the love of God. Thank God for putting these people on your path. Ask your Guardian Angel to disclose to you quickly what lessons God wants you to learn from your enemies.

Bless God's Wisdom. Acknowledge His Lordship. Trust that He will bring good out of your life and all the circumstances He has allowed to befall you. Such trust empowers angels to help you mightily.

Praise God's Kindness and Generosity to you.

Focus on the beauty and goodness with which He has enriched your life. Always expect great joy with the help of angels.

4. Develop the Spirit of Prayer

To accomplish this goal, reread *Angel Power*, especially those sections that resonate with your life journey today. Ponder the changes that Angel Power brought into the lives of those whose stories are shared in this book. Pray for the light to recognize and accept God's Will for you. Confer with your Guardian Angel and the Angels of the Nine Choirs about everything you think, say, and do.

5. Develop the habit of sacred silence

Empty your mind, quiet your imagination, silence your lips, close your eyes, fold your hands, and sit quietly and erectly at least three times each day. Wait patiently for God. He comes when you least expect Him.

Speak as little as possible always. Speak only to bless. Ask your Guardian Angel to communicate your needs and desires to the Guardian Angels of the other people in your life. The angels are far better communicators between humans than the wisdom of our present stage of awareness recognizes.

6. Each day find someone to help

No matter how difficult your own life may be, there is always someone less fortunate than you. You are most like the angels when you are an instrument of God's Love and Mercy to yourself and to others. Discipline yourself strictly to seek out someone each day to consciously help in some way. Never let the sun set on a day when you have helped no one.

As a friend of angels you are called from all eternity to be an instrument of love and mercy to those around you. Simple gifts are always appreciated by angels. Does someone in your family need help? Does someone in your place of employment need gracious affirmation? Does your neighbor need help? Always be the *prudent* Good Samaritan. There are those whose life circumstances are so bleak that they have absolutely no one to give them time, a kind word, a smile, a courteous gesture or response, or even a hug.

As you come to know angels well, many people will be placed upon your path. Bless those who cross your path with a handshake, a glorious smile, or even a hug. True friends of angels give amazing "hugs": jobs, education, hospitality, medical, legal or accounting assistance, food, clothing, shelter. Much is expected of those to whom much is given. (Hospitals, nursing homes, schools, orphanages, prisons, soup kitchens, relief centers for victims of natural disaster and countless other institutions depend on the generosity of volunteers.)

7. Be gracious to God's poor

They are poor because many people do not share. Give away everything you do not need with a generous heart filled with love. Then you will be free. You will be happy, and God's Angels will fill you full. Be sensitive first to the needs of your family and friends. Then go out to all the world. Fill them with God's Love and Generosity. In your newfound freedom you will be a vehicle of His Love and His Joy and His Generosity. Through you God will fill the world with His Graciousness. Be a faithful friend of angels. Be like angels. Be angels of God's Love and Mercy to one another.

8. Obey God peacefully and be filled always with trust

Trust Him totally in every little decision. Then the big decisions are easy. Always see how His Beloved Jesus obeyed His Will. See any "crucifixion" you must undergo as fleeting steps to a glorious and newfound life. Use the strength of God's Faithful Angels to be a good and humble servant. Work with angels. Love with angels. Sing with angels. Play with angels. Live always with angels.

9. Open your spiritual eyes and your spiritual ears

Ask the angels to help you to look for God everywhere. Call to Him. Cry to Him. Sing to Him. Bless Him. Persevere. Send messages, petitions, thoughts, desires, and needs to God through your Guardian Angel and all the Angels of the Nine Choirs.

10. AWAIT GOD

As you acquire Angel Power, expect great things! God is all around you. His love fills your world. You are His Treasure. The angels see His Face at all times. Pray fervently with the angels that God grants you eyes to see Him in the world, ears to hear Him in the world, and a heart that beats for Him alone. Those who seek God find Him and His Kingdom of Heaven, even on earth.

Each new day that you have is a glorious journey with the angels. Yesterdays are past, and tomorrows have no reality where the angels rule. Their Kingdom is yours, their Eternal Now is yours, for Angel Power transports you into the very Heart of God.

Meditation

See.

*When you see who you are, dear little ones of My Covenant, how
   happy you shall be.*

How sorrowful your own sins will make you.

*Fast now, dear little ones, that you might be freed of the darkness
   of lies.*

See lies as snakes.

See them entwine themselves around you.

See them choke off the life-giving air of truth.

Cast them off, My Little Ones, by prayer and fasting.

It is only in fasting that the snakes of lies unsnarl from you.

*Fasting, combined with prayer, will free you, My Little Ones,
   from the snakes of lies.*

*When you are no longer in their power, you shall be able to see
   Truth.*

The Truth will set you free from the bondage of the Evil One.
How I long for all My children to be free.

I am the Liberator. There is no other.
Come to Me, My Little Ones, for I am your Father.
My arms are outstretched.
All of Paradise awaits your arrival.

Prayer

God our Father, please give me
Eyes to see You in the world,
Ears to hear You in the world,
And a heart that beats
For You alone.

Give me hands that serve Your children.
Give me feet that carry Your Will to the four winds
All for the love of You, Dear Father,
In time and in eternity. Amen

Angel Power Now: Daily Meditations

Thirty Daily Meditations to Ponder on the Path to Enlightenment

1. True wisdom is steeped in Angel Power.

2. With true wisdom we see our Father's hand in every circumstance of our lives.

3. I Am who Am. My love guides and comforts each of My children. My love resides in My Faithful children, who, through My Compassion, comfort and love My Suffering children.

4. Suffering is often a blessed gift of our Father. Suffering is a test of a soul's faithfulness. There is no suffering a soul experiences which our Father does not experience too.

5. Suffering brings peace. Suffering brings happiness. Suffering brings freedom. In suffering we shed our attachments to the earth and to the things of the earth, which are transitory.

6. I Myself call My children to Myself. I free them from their bondage. I bring them along the path of My Son Jesus to Myself.

6. Each soul must pass through the valley of suffering to come to My Waiting Arms.

7. Those who comfort the afflicted will be comforted.

8. Those who carry the burdens of another are one with the angels in My Will.

9. Though you must walk in the valley of darkness for a while, know that I am here.

10. I never reward iniquity. You must not eat of the fruit of the poison tree. It will make you sick. You will lose your discernment. You will not be

able to hear My Voice. You will be unable to see Me in the world. The poison tree is lies, deceit, stolen goods.

11. When you come to Me in truth and humility, I will set you free.

12. Be very careful, My children. Be at peace. Wear My Strength. Wear My Courage. Wear My Fortitude. Know that I alone am God. I alone judge. I alone understand the human heart. Though you must walk in the valley of tears, know that I am with you. Your tears are My Tears. Your sufferings are My Sufferings.

13. You must trust My Will. I alone know all things. I alone am God. Idle curiosity offends Me. Idle speculation offends Me. Worry offends Me. Conflict offends Me. Surrender into My Waiting Arms.

14. I AM TRUTH. When you deviate from My Will, you live in darkness. Darkness begets darkness. The longer you live in and adhere to ways that are not My Will, the farther from My Will you wander.

15. See how Jesus lived! See how Mary lived! I have given you a pattern to follow.

16. See all the beautiful things of the world. Their presence in your life is My Gift to you. Praise Me, My children. See My Beauty in the world and preserve it.

17. Experience My Presence in the world. I never leave you. I am always with you.

18. Sinful patterns need awareness to be changed. Pray for the awareness of sinful habits and patterns. Desires for the allures of the world lead My children to sin. Much of the suffering of My children is due to sin.

19. When people share feelings of nonlove, they all sin. The bond of charity is broken. Then comes alienation, disdain, and ostracism.

20. To share feelings of nonlove requires judgment of one another. No human in a body can judge another human.

21. Humanity's lack of love for one another is the cause of suffering in My World. It is through and with My Love that you are able to love one another.

22. All human laws must have love for Me, for My Ways, as their underpinning.

23. Selfishness begets selfishness unless My Grace intervenes.

24. Be at peace, My children. I smite. I bind up. My anger cleanses. It restores repentant hearts. Be at peace, My children. All will be well.

25. Remain in My Love, My children. The way will be shown to you. Keep your hearts pure. Obey My Commands to you. My Kingdom is a kingdom of Love. My chastisements prepare My children to live in that Kingdom.

26. Evil is action devoid of me. It is through love that all evil is conquered.

27. Love closes all wounds. Love heals. Love frees. The love is Me.

28. My children, by their faithfulness to My Will, bring My Presence to all their actions. Pray and sacrifice. Free My World from darkness, from blindness to My Presence.

29. In Me and through Me and with Me all things and all dreams are well. I am the longing of all hearts, the object of all dreams, the source and goal of all that is.

30. Live in peace. Live in joy. Live in love. Experience My Providence in your life. Experience My Presence in your life. Love and serve your brothers and sisters in Me and through Me and with Me. My children, I am inviting you to be fellow servants with Me. That is true Angel Power.

Novena

IN HONOR OF THE NINE CHOIRS OF ANGELS*

Glory be to the Father and to the Son and to the Holy Spirit
As it was in the beginning, is now, and ever shall be
World without end. Amen

*This novena has proven to be highly effective in times of stress or emergency. Repeat nine times in honor of each of the Nine Choirs of Angels, nine times during the day.

Who may go up to the mountain of the LORD?
Who can stand in his holy place?
"The clean of hand and pure of heart,
who are not devoted to idols,
who have not sworn falsely.
They will receive blessings from the LORD,
and justice from their saving God.
Such are the people that love the Lord,
that seek the face of the God of Jacob."

—Psalms 24:3–6

Epilogue

Even the littlest flowers
on the remotest plains tremble
in expectation
as the winds of change slightly
stir the memory of all creation
for days of long ago
when purity, holiness, and peace
reigned upon the earth's sweet face.
Bloodstained, pock-marked, contaminated and toxic,
the earth awaits
the glorious return of the Savior,
who will make all things new.
The Creator is the patient, Enduring, loving
Parent who hovers over creation
constantly caring,
constantly nurturing.
The despot frets over creation,
ever jealous, ever officious,

ever stirring up, ever

distorting, condemned to endure

the unending praise

and honor and glory

that spontaneously rise up to its Creator

from the earth's sweet breast.

Notwithstanding a constant seething

Belch of hatred, animosity,

and vengeance that emits from the evil one's bowels

to deface the

Beauty, Harmony,

and tranquillity of creation,

the earth spins on

in countless

mornings of hope.

Endnotes

Chapter One

1. Jean Daniélou, S.J., *The Angels and Their Mission* (Westminster, Md.: Newman Press, 1957), p. 31.

2. Ibid.

3. Ibid.

4. Ibid.

5. Paul J. Glenn, *A Tour of the Summa* (Rockford, Ill.: Tan Books, 1978) pp. 89–90.

6. Thomas Aquinas, *Summa Theologiae: A Concise Translation* (Westminster, Md.: Christian Classics, 1989), pp. 99–102.

7. Glenn, *Tour of the Summa*, pp. 89–93.

8. Ibid., p. 91.

9. Ibid.

10. Pope Gregory I, *Forty Gospel Homilies: Gregory the Great* (Kalamazoo, Mich.: Cistercian Publications, 1990), p. 285.

11. Benedict J. Groeschel, C.F.R. *A Still, Small Voice* (San Francisco: Ignatius Press, 1993), p. 19.

12. Jean Baptiste Saint-Jure and Blessed Claude De La Colombière, *Trustful Surrender to Divine Providence* (Rockford, Ill.: Tan Books, 1983), p. 19.

13. Thomas Aquinas. *Summa*, 1, q. 19, a. 4; cited in Saint-Jure and De La Colombière, *Trustful Surrender*, p. 13.

14. *Newsweek*, August 1, 1994.

15. *Newsweek*, March 28, 1994.

Chapter Four

1. Pope Gregory I, italicized portion of extract from Thomas Aquinas, *Summa Theologiae: A Concise Translation* (Westminster, Md.: Christian Classics, 1989), p. 157.

2. *Saint Michael and the Archangels* (Rockford, Ill.: Tan Books, 1983), p. 64.

3. The author makes no representation that the alleged words and facts available about apparitions are totally accurate, or that they even occurred. In many cases, including this one, I have tried to recreate the words of the Angels or other Divine Beings, since no written record of these words exists. Data that would stand up to the scientific scrutiny of the twentieth century did not exist in prior generations. The words, recollections, and beliefs chronicled in private revelation are part of the treasure contained in the oral history of the faith.

4. Adapted from Robert J. Fox, *The World and Work of the Holy Angels* (Alexandria, S.D.: Fatima Family Apostolate, 1991), p. 55. This work is an invaluable resource for those who wish to study the angels. The words of the archangel are based on the legend of San Miguel del Milagro.

5. Ibid, pp. 55–60.

Chapter Five

1. Janice T. Connell, *The Triumph of the Immaculate Heart* (Santa Barbara, Calif.: Queenship Publishing, 1993), pp. 34–37, adapted for this volume with the gracious permission of the publishers.

2. See note 3, chapter 4.

3. Saint Francis of Sales, *Introduction to the Devout Life* (Rockford, Ill.: Tan Books, 1984), p. xv.

4. Paul O'Sullivan, O.P. *All About the Angels* (Rockford, Ill.: Tan Books, 1990), p. 140.

Chapter Six

1. Paul J. Glenn, *A Tour of the Summa* (Rockford, Ill.: Tan Books, 1978), p. 89.

2. Some of the "facts" about the angels are gathered from the revelations made to Mechtilde, the Ancilla Domini, gathered from her writings by Friederich von Lama and contained in *The Angels: Our God-Given Companions and Servants* (Washington, N.J.: The Blue Army, 1989).

3. Ibid., p. 7.

4. Glenn, *Tour of the Summa*, p. 89.

5. Ibid., p. 93.

6. Ibid.

7. Von Lama, *Angels*, p. 7.

8. Ibid., p. 14.

9. Ibid., p. 12.

10. Ibid., p. 14.

11. Thomas Aquinas, *Summa Theologiae: A Concise Translation* (Westminster, Md.: Christian Classics, 1989), p. 158.

12. Cardinal Charles Journet, introduction to Georges Huber, *My Angel Will Go Before You* (Westminster, Md.: Christian Classics, 1983), pp. 11–15.

Chapter Seven

1. Thomas Aquinas, *Summa Theologiae: A Concise Translation* (Westminster, Md.: Christian Classics, 1989), p. 157.

2. Ibid., p. 96.

3. Ibid.

4. Ibid., pp. 95–98.

5. Ibid., pp. 99–102.

6. A Sacrament is an outward sign instituted by Christ to give grace.

7. Friederich von Lama, ed., *The Angels: Our God-Given Companions and Servants* (Washington, N.J.: The Blue Army, 1989), p. 15.

8. See Pope John Paul II, *The Splendor of Truth: Encyclical Letter* (Boston: Saint Paul Books & Media, 1993), p. 9. "The splendor of truth shines forth in all the works of the Creator and, in a special way, in man, created in the image and likeness of God (cf. Gen. 1:26). Truth enlightens man's intelligence and shapes his freedom, leading him to know and love the Lord."

Chapter Eight

1. Janice T. Connell, *Visions of the Children* (New York: St. Martin's Press, 1992), pp. 155–80.

2. Thomas Aquinas, *Summa Theologiae: A Concise Translation* (Westminster, Md.: Christian Classics, 1989), pp. 158–59.

3. Pope John Paul II, *The Splendor of Truth: Encyclical Letter* (Boston: Saint Paul Books & Media, 1993), p. 9.

4. M. Scott Peck, M.D., *People of the Lie* (New York: Simon & Schuster, 1983), p. 222.

5. Thomas Aquinas, *Summa Theologiae*, pp. 82–85, 96, 101–103, 158.

6. Janice T. Connell, *Queen of the Cosmos* (Orleans, Mass.: Paraclete Press, 1990), pp. 9–32; and *Visions of the Children*, pp. 39–74.

7. Blessed M. Faustina Kowalska, *Divine Mercy in My Soul: The Diary* (Stockbridge, Mass.: Marian Press, 1990), pp. 296, 297.

Chapter Nine

1. Venerable Mary of Agreda, *Mystical City of God*, vol. 1, *The Conception* (Washington, N.J.: Ave Maria Institute, 1971), pp. 83–124.

2. Ibid.

3. *Saint Michael and the Archangels* (Rockford, Ill.: Tan Books, 1983), p. 42.

Chapter Ten

1. Robert J. Fox, *The World and Work of the Holy Angels* (Alexandria, S.D.: Fatima Family Apostolate, 1991), pp. 12–19.

2. Jean Daniélou, *The Angels and Their Mission: According to the Fathers of the Church* (Westminster, Md.: Newman Press, 1957), p. 31.

3. Paul J. Glenn, *A Tour of the Summa* (Rockford, Ill.: Tan Books, 1978), p. 54.

4. Pope Gregory I, *Forty Gospel Homilies: Gregory the Great* (Kalamazoo, Mich.: Cistercian Publications, 1990), p. 285.

5. Ibid., p. 291.

6. Ibid., p. 289.

7. Venerable Mary of Agreda, *Mystical City of God*, vol. 1, *The Conception* (Washington, N.J.: Ave Maria Institute, 1971), pp. 24–31.

8. Friederich von Lama, comp., *The Angels: Our God-Given Companions and Servants* (Washington, N.J.: The Blue Army, 1989), p. 5.

9. Blessed M. Faustina Kowalska, *Divine Mercy in My Soul: The Diary* (Stockbridge, Mass.: Marian Press, 1987).

10. Ibid. That is not to imply that all those who are entrusted with special missions are accompanied by Seraphim. The angel support staff assigned to human projects is determined by God alone. The Mission of Divine Mercy, as outlined in Blessed Faustina Kowalska's *Diary*, is of remarkable apocalyptic dimensions and chronicles the spiritual reality of the times leading up to and following World War II.

11. D.D.C. Pochin Mould, *The Angels* (Chicago, Ill.: Clarentian Publications), pp. 13–15. This and other resources were made available through the graciousness of Thomas King, S.J., and Richard McSorley, S.J., of Georgetown University; G. McGinity, of Dublin, Ireland; C. Antonicelli, of Washington, D.C.; Vicka Ivankovic, Ivanka Elez, and Jelena Vasilj, of Medjugorje; John Haffert, The Blue Army and the 101 Foundation; Sue Ellis, of Surrey, England; Claire and Janet Schafer, of Santa Barbara, Calif.; Dominic Berardino, S.C.R.C.; C. Carroll Carter; Tom Petrisco; Don and Debbie Ralph. Thanks most of all to Mary Christian, whose precious questions about the angels began this book.

12. Certain groups of worshipers commit their lives and resources to praise and adoration of God on behalf of the entire community. They endeavor to unite their human life on earth to the angelic life of the Seraphim and Cherubim.

13. Pope Gregory I, *Forty Gospel Homilies*, p. 288.

14. Ibid.

Chapter Eleven

1. Paul J. Glenn, *A Tour of the Summa* (Rockford, Ill.: Tan Books, 1978), p. 90.

2. Pope Gregory I, *Forty Gospel Homilies: Gregory the Great* (Kalamazoo, Mich.: Cistercian Publications, 1989), p. 288.

3. Paul O'Sullivan, O.P. *All About the Angels* (Rockville, Ill.: Tan Books, 1990), p. 14.

4. Pope Gregory I, *Forty Gospel Homilies*, p. 288.

5. Ibid.

6. Ibid.

7. Glenn, *Tour of the Summa*, pp. 87–91.

8. Taken from the microfilm of the original published journal, the *National Tribune*, vol. 4, no. 12 (Dec. 1880), which is contained in the Library of Congress, Washington, D.C., through the graciousness of the Honorable Margaret Mary Heckler.

Chapter Twelve

1. Pope Gregory I, pp. 285–287.

2. W. Doyle Gilligan, ed., *Devotion to the Holy Angels* (Houston: Lumen Christi Press, 1990), pp. 7–8.

3. Paul O'Sullivan, O.P., *All About the Angels* (Rockville, Ill.: Tan Books, 1990), p. 14.

4. Paul J. Glenn, *A Tour of the Summa* (Rockford, Ill.: Tan Books, 1978), p. 46.

5. Blessed Josemaria Escriva, *The Way* (Manila, Phil.: Sinag-Tala Publishers, 1982), p. 192.

6. Billy Graham, *Angels* (Dallas: Word Publishing, 1975), p. 83.

7. *The Koran, The Preliminary Discourse*, ed. by George Sale (London: T. Maiden, Sherbourne Lane, 1801), p. 94.

8. Jean Daniélou, *The Angels and Their Mission: According to the Fathers of the Church* (Westminster, Md.: Christian Classics, 1957), pp. 101–102.

9. Ibid., p. 96.

10. Ibid., p. 99.

11. Daniélou, op. cit., quoting Origen (*Hom. in Num.*, 25, 5), p. 100.

12. Daniélou, op. cit., quoting Origen (*Hom. in Num.*, 5, 3), p. 111.

13. Daniélou, op. cit., quoting Eusebius (*Comm. in Is.*, 66), p. 111.

Chapter Fourteen

1. Saint Ignatius of Loyola, *The Spiritual Exercises* (New York: Doubleday Image Books, 1989).

2. Ibid.

3. M. Scott Peck, *People of the Lie* (New York: Simon & Schuster, 1983), pp. 250–53.

4. "My eighty years' experience have helped me to see the truth that the purpose of life is holiness. All else is deceit or a waste of time." Richard McSorley, S.J., address delivered at Georgetown University, October 2, 1994, the Feast of the Guardian Angels.

Selected Bibliography

Anderson, Joan Wester. *Where Angels Walk*. New York: Ballantine Books, 1992.

Aquinas, Thomas. *Summa Theologica*, 5 vols. Westminster, Md.: Christian Classics, 1981.

————. *Summa Theologiae: A Concise Translation*. Edited by Timothy McDermott. Westminster, Md.: Christian Classics, 1989.

Augustine, Saint. *The Confessions*. Garden City, N.Y.: Doubleday Image Books, 1960.

Bennett, William J. *The Book of Virtues*. New York: Simon & Schuster, 1993.

Berendt, John. *Midnight in the Garden of Good and Evil*. New York: Random House, 1994.

Birgitta of Sweden, Saint and Queen. *Birgitta: Life and Selected Revelations*. New York: Paulist Press, 1990.

Brown, Michael H. *Prayer of the Warrior*. Milford, Ohio: Faith Publishing Co., 1992.

Bryant, Christopher. *The Heart in Pilgrimage*. New York: Seabury Press, 1980.

Burghardt, Walter J., S.J. *Sir, We Would Like to See Jesus*. Ramsey, N.J.: Paulist Press, 1982.

Burnham, Sophie. *Angel Letters*. New York: Ballantine Books, 1991.

——. *A Book of Angels*. New York: Ballantine Books, 1990.

Burrows, Ruth. *Fire upon the Earth*. Denville, N.J.: Dimension Books, 1981.

Catherine of Sienna, Saint. *The Dialogue*. Ramsey, N.J.: Paulist Press, 1980.

Caussade, Jean-Pierre De, *The Joy of Full Surrender*. Orleans, Mass.: Paraclete Press, 1986.

Ciszek, Walter J., S.J. *With God in Russia*. Garden City, N.Y.: Doubleday Image Books, 1966.

Connell, Janice T. *Queen of the Cosmos*. Introduction by Robert Faricy, S.J. Orleans, Mass.: Paraclete Press, 1990.

——. *The Triumph of the Immaculate Heart*. Introduction by Rene Laurentin. Santa Barbara, Calif.: Queenship Publishing, 1993.

——. *Visions of the Children*. Introduction by Robert Faricy, S.J. New York: St. Martin's Press, 1992.

Covey, Stephen R. *The 7 Habits of Highly Effective People*. New York: Simon & Schuster, 1989.

Daniélou, Jean, S.J., *The Angels and Their Mission: According to the Fathers of the Church*. Westminster, Md.: Newman Press, 1957.

Dossey, Larry, M.D. *Healing Words*. San Francisco: Harper, 1993.

Dubay, Thomas, S.M. *Fire Within*. San Francisco: Ignatius Press, 1989.

Dupre, Louis, and James A. Wiseman, O.S.B., eds. *Light from Light: An Anthology of Christian Mysticism*. New York: Paulist Press, 1988.

Eadie, Betty J. Foreword by Melvin Morse, M.D. *Embraced by the Light*. Placerville, Calif.: Gold Leaf Press, 1992.

Escriva, Blessed Josemaria. *The Way*. Manila, Phil.: Sinag-Tala Publishers, 1982.

Faricy, Robert, S.J. *The Lord's Dealing: The Primacy of the Feminine in Christian Spirituality*. New York: Paulist Press, 1988.

————. *Praying for Inner Healing*. New York: Paulist Press, 1979.

Faricy, Robert, S.J., and Lucy Rooney, S.D.N. *The Contemplative Way of Prayer*. Ann Arbor, Mich.: Servant Books, 1986.

Fox, Robert J., *The World and Work of the Holy Angels*. Alexandria, S.D.: Fatima Family Apostolate, 1991.

Francis of Sales, Saint. *Introduction to the Devout Life*. Rockford, Ill.: Tan Books, 1984.

Gilligan, W. Doyle, ed. *Devotion to the Holy Angels*. Houston: Lumen Christi Press, 1990.

Glenn, Paul J. *A Tour of the Summa*. Rockford, Ill.: Tan Books, 1978.

Graham, Billy. *Angels*. Dallas: Word Publishing, 1975.

Gregory I, Pope. *Forty Gospel Homilies: Gregory the Great*. Translated by David Hurst. Kalamazoo, Mich.: Cistercian Publications, 1990.

Groeschel, Benedict J., C.F.R. *A Still, Small Voice*. San Francisco: Ignatius Press, 1993.

Heine, Max. *Equipping Men for Spiritual Battle*. Ann Arbor, Mich.: Servant Books, 1993.

Huber, Georges. *My Angel Will Go Before You*. Introduction by Cardinal Charles Journet. Westminster, Md.: Christian Classics, 1983.

Ignatius of Loyola, Saint. *The Spiritual Exercises*. Translated by Anthony Mohola. New York: Doubleday Image Books, 1989.

John of the Cross, Saint. *Selected Writings*. Translated by Kieran Kavanaugh, O.C.D. New York: Paulist Press, 1987.

John Paul II, Pope. *The Splendor of Truth: Encyclical Letter*. Boston: Saint Paul Books & Media, 1993.

Johnson, William, ed. *The Cloud of Unknowing*. New York: Doubleday Image Books, 1973.

Julian of Norwich. *Showings*. Introduction by Edmund Cooledge, O.S.A., and James Walsh, S.J. New York: Paulist Press, 1978.

Kowalska, Blessed M. Faustina. *Divine Mercy in My Soul: The Diary*. Stockbridge, Mass.: Marian Press, 1990.

Kushner, Harold S. *When Bad Things Happen to Good People*. New York: Avon Books, 1981.

Lewis, C. S. *The Screwtape Letters*. New York.: Macmillan, 1943.

Lord, Bob, and Penny. *Heavenly Army of Angels*. Birmingham, Ala.: Journeys of Faith Publications, 1991.

Lymann, Sanford M. *The Seven Deadly Sins: Society and Evil*. New York: St. Martin's Press, 1978.

MacNutt, Francis. *Healing*. Notre Dame, Ind.: Ave Maria Press, 1974.

McSorley, Richard, S.J. *New Testament Basis for Peace Making*. Scottsdale, Pa.: Herald Press, 1985.

Maloney, George A., S.J. *Called to Intimacy.: Living in the Indwelling Presence*. New York: Alba House, 1983.

Mandino, Og. *The Twelfth Angel*. New York: Ballantine Books, 1993.

Margolies, Morris B. *A Gathering of Angels*. New York: Ballantine Books, 1994.

Marshall, Peter, and David Manuel. *The Light and the Glory: Did God Have a Plan for America?* Tarrytown, N.Y.: Fleming H. Revell, 1977.

Mary of Agreda, The Venerable. *Mystical City of God.* 4 vols. Washington, N.J.: Ave Maria Institute, 1971.

Montfort, Saint Louis De. *God Alone: The Collected Writings of St. Louis De Montfort.* Washington, N.J.: The Blue Army, 1989.

Moore, Thomas, *Care of the Soul.* New York: HarperCollins, 1992.

Morse, Melvin, M.D. *Transformed by the Light.* New York: Ivy Books, 1992.

Most, William G. *Our Father's Plan.* Manassas, Va.: Trinity Communications, 1988.

Muto, Susan A. *Pathways of Spiritual Living.* Garden City, N.Y.: Doubleday Image Books, 1984.

New American Bible, The. Nashville, Tenn.: Catholic Bible Press, div. of Thomas Nelson, 1987.

Nikodimos, Saint, and Saint Makarios of Corinth. *The Philokalia.* 4 vols. London: Faber and Faber, 1984.

Opus Sanctorum Angelorum. *Newsletter.* Casa Regina Pacis / Rua do Anjo, 5. 2495 Fatima, Portugal. Tel.: (049) 532280. Fax: (049) 531172.

Origen. *An Exhortation to Martyrdom, Prayer, First Principles: Book IV.* New York: Paulist Press, 1979.

O'Connor, Edward D., C.S.C. *The Catholic Vision.* Huntington, Ind.: Our Sunday Visitor Publishing Division, 1992.

O'Sullivan, Paul, O.P. *All About the Angels.* Rockford, Ill.: Tan Books, 1990.

Paine, Randall Paine, O.R.C. *The Angels Are Waiting.* St. Paul, Minn.: The Leaflet Missal, 1988.

Peck, M. Scott. *People of the Lie*. New York: Simon & Schuster, 1983.

———. *The Road Less Traveled*. New York: Simon & Schuster, 1981.

Ponchin Mould, D.D.C. *The Angels*. Chicago, Ill.: Claretian Publications, 1968.

Powell, John, S.J. *Fully Human, Fully Alive*. Allen, Tex.: Tabor, 1976.

Prince, Derek. *Blessing or Curse: You Can Choose*. Tarrytown, N.Y.: Chosen Books, 1990.

Saint Michael and the Angels. Rockford, Ill.: Tan Books, 1983.

Saint-Jure, Jean Baptiste, S.J., and Blessed Claude De La Colombière, S.J. *Trustful Surrender to Divine Providence*. Rockford, Ill.: Tan Books, 1983.

Sanford, Agnes. *The Healing Gifts of the Spirit*. Philadelphia: Harper and Row, 1966.

Sanford, John A. *The Kingdom Within*. San Francisco: Harper and Row, 1987.

Scanlan, Michael, T.O.R. *Appointment with God*. Steubenville, Ohio: Franciscan University Press, 1987.

Scanlan, Michael, T.O.R., and Randall J. Cirner. *Deliverance from Evil Spirits*. Ann Arbor, Mich.: Servant Books, 1980.

Schouppe, F.X., S.J. *The Dogma of Hell*. Rockford, Ill.: Tan Books, 1989.

Scupoli, Dom Lorenzo. *The Spiritual Combat and a Treatise on Peace of Soul*. Rockford, Ill.: Tan Books, 1990.

Teresa of Avila. *The Interior Castle*. Translated by Kieran Kavanaugh, O.C.D. New York: Paulist Press, 1979.

———. *The Way of Perfection*. Translated and edited by Allison Peers. New York: Doubleday Image Books, 1964.

Theresa of Lisieux, Saint. *The Autobiography: The Story of a Soul*. New York: Doubleday, 1957.

Van Kaam, Adrien, C.S.Sp. *The Mystery of Transforming Love*. Denville, N.J.: Dimension Books, 1981.

————. *The Roots of Christian Joy*. Denville, N.J.: Dimension Books, 1985.

Von Lama, Friederich, ed. *The Angels: Our God-Given Companions and Servants*. Washington, N.J.: The Blue Army, 1989.

Walsh, Michael, ed. *Butler's Lives of the Saints*. Foreword by Cardinal Basil Hume, O.S.B. San Francisco: Harper and Row, 1984.

Weil, Simone. *Waiting for God*. New York: Harper and Row, 1951.

More information is available from the author concerning the angels and their presence in our lives.

Do you have experiences with the angels that you would like to share?

If you are interested in writing to the author, please address all correspondence to

Janice T. Connell
Two Gateway Center
Suite 620
Pittsburgh, Pennsylvania 15222

Picture Credits

p. xiv: *The Angels' Trumpets*, Culver Pictures

p. 8: *The Heavenly Choir*, Culver Pictures

p. 20: *Tobias and the Angel* by Cima da Conegliano, Alinari, Art Resource, NY

p. 30: *Warrior Angels*, Culver Pictures

p. 48: *The Angel of the Resurrection*, Culver Pictures

p. 54: *Sarah and the Angel*, Art Resource, NY

p. 64: *The Guardian Angel* by Zampieri, Culver Pictures

p. 66: *Three Angels*, Duomo, Spoleto, Alinari/Art Resource, NY

p. 70: *St. Michael* by Piero della Francesca, reproduced by courtesy of the Trustees, The National Gallery, London

p. 86: *Madonna in the Rose Garden* by Lochner, Foto Marburg/Art Resource, NY

p. 98: *The Guardian Angel* by Von Kaulbach, Culver Pictures

p. 110: *Guardian Angels*, Culver Pictures

p. 116: *Christ in Gethsemane*, Culver Pictures

p. 134: *Guardian Angels*, Culver Pictures

p. 144: *St. Michael and the Dragon*, artist unknown, The Metropolitan Museum of Art, Rogers Fund, 1912 (12.192)

p. 162: *The Guardian Angel* by Tessier, Culver Pictures

p. 180: *Group of Angels* by Torriti, Culver Pictures

p. 192: *The Perussis Altarpiece* (detail, Angel), unknown French painter, The Metropolitan Museum of Art, Purchase, 1954, Bequest of Mary Metmore Shively, in memory of her husband, Henry Shively, 1954 (54.195)

p. 196: *The First Law* by Dore, Culver Pictures

p. 202: *Appearance of the Virgin to St. Bernard*, Alinari/Art Resource, NY

p. 216: *The Advent Angel*, Culver Pictures

p. 220: *Christmas Angels*, Culver Pictures

p. 230: *Elias and the Angel*, Culver Pictures

p. 242: *An Angel Appears to Joshua*, Culver Pictures

p. 274: *The Annunciation* by Botticelli, The Metropolitan Museum of Art, Robert Lehman Collection, 1975 (1975.1.74)